DRI
BOTH WAYS

Dylan Moore is a writer, teacher and editor of the Institute of Welsh Affairs' magazine, *the welsh agenda*. He serves on the executive committee of Wales PEN Cymru, and is a Creative Wales Hay Festival International Fellow. He lives with his family in Newport.

DRIVING HOME BOTH WAYS

DYLAN MOORE

To/ Pam,

Enjoy !

[signature]

PARTHIAN

Parthian, Cardigan SA43 1ED
www.parthianbooks.com
First published in 2018
© Dylan Moore 2018
ISBN 978-1-912109-99-9
Editor: Adam Somerset
Cover design: www.theundercard.co.uk
Typeset by Elaine Sharples
Printed in EU by Pulsio SARL
Published with the financial support of the Welsh Books Council.
British Library Cataloguing in Publication Data
A cataloguing record for this book is available from the British Library.

The true nationalist is a world citizen: the windows of his mind face the four corners of the world, and the doors of his sympathies are with all the families of the earth.
David Miall Edwards

It's not where you're from
It's not where you're at
It's not where you've been
It's where you're between
**Super Furry Animals,
'The International Language of Screaming'**

for Chantelle

CONTENTS

Becoming Welsh in '99

Cardiff, 2005

The native name for Wales, Cymru, is related to the English word compatriot; the name the English gave 'Wales' comes from Latin for foreigner. Throughout centuries of complex history between two nations who have fought, according to one historian, 'like cats in a sack', two things have remained the same: the English have tried to keep themselves separate from the Welsh, and the Welsh wouldn't have it any other way. For reasons geographical, historical and cultural, a huge part of being Welsh is being 'not English'. And yet this is the story of how I became, or, as I'll try to explain, *realised I was* Welsh.

The story starts years earlier than that, when as a child growing up in rural Wales, miles from the nearest shop or pub or post office, I came across a book given to my dad – a Liverpudlian in exile – by his brother still living in Liverpool. It was a romanticised, nostalgic collection of black and white photographs and fragments of text evoking the people and places of a city half-forgotten. I loved looking through the book with its faded pictures of civic buildings, cathedrals and flat-capped football crowds. I loved especially the black kids peering out of shop doorways and the haggard faces of dockers and market traders, imagining them my ancestors. I listened to my dad's stories of playing in 'jiggers' and bombed-out houses and thought it much more glamorous than sharpening sticks and making dens in the shadow of Pen y Fan.

I didn't fit in. I was seeking something all the kids I played with had as birthright. There were Prices and Davieses and three families worth of Powells, none of whom were remotely related, so far as they knew. I was still English at this point (I've since had a nationality transplant). A mum from Gloucestershire and a Scouse dad doesn't give you much claim to being Welsh. Maybe perversely, I was seeking identity through being an outsider. As time went by, I came to realise that even if outsiderdom has its merits, a sense of belonging is a far more satisfactory type of identity.

By twist of catchment areas, I ended up having to travel twelve miles to secondary school, further into the identity hinterlands of border country. Some of my friends living the wrong side of the hills couldn't pick up S4C, and here Welshness – whether it was a language, an accent or support of a sports team – was seen as something to be rid of before it dragged you under. I won the Eisteddfod with a poem about the demise of mining, but that wasn't our country, or our generation. The Wales of that poem, gloomily titled 'The Wheel Doesn't Turn Any More', was old newsreel and hackneyed stereotype. We all dropped Welsh at age fourteen and turned our eyes eastward.

By Sixth Form, it was taken as inevitable that all of us – my clique of friends, bound together by academic prowess, a love of Blur and The Stone Roses and a mutual disdain for Mid Wales and its lack of hipness – would escape to far-flung universities to reinvent ourselves and never return. We decided, in the full-flushed arrogance of youth, that we would go to Oxbridge, drink Pimms, talk shit and become cabinet ministers. Four of us applied: three to Oxford, one to Cambridge. None of us got in.

There were different reasons for all of the rejections, I'm sure, but it was now obvious to me that the Establishment did not exactly give two hoots about scruffy-haired seventeen-year-olds from some backwater comprehensive school with a very-hard-to-pronounce Welsh name, especially those whose interview suit consisted of a fifteen-quid Oxfam jacket and a pair of old school trousers that had been worn out working in a fish-and-chip shop all summer, and who named John Steinbeck as their favourite author but had not read *The Grapes of Wrath*, and who tried to make up for it by lying and saying they had read *Cannery Row*. In the same week as my disastrous Oxford interview – the first week of December 1997 – I went on an Open Day in Cardiff, making up the numbers on my application form because it was the nearest decent English Literature degree.

Cardiff had, until then, only figured on the margins of my consciousness. It was the capital of Wales, but at that time – pre-Millennium Stadium, pre-Cool Cymru, pre-devolution – and from where I lived, it was just a big town to go shopping in, like Swansea or Hereford. The problem wasn't its lack of glamour: I could cope without that. It simply lacked the mystique of cities further afield. But when I finally got there, in the autumn of 1998, after the inevitable rejections from elsewhere, it seemed the whole city was celebrating my arrival. Between receiving the letter offering me a place at Cardiff University and my first pint in the Talybont Halls of Residence, Catatonia and Stereophonics had taken over the charts, Graham Henry was hailed as The Great Redeemer and Ron Davies was in the process of delivering devolved government. They even built a stadium in my honour. Almost overnight, Cardiff came of age as Europe's Youngest Capital and I discovered I was Welsh after all.

Nationality had suddenly assumed an importance I had barely ascribed to it before. Starting university is like appearing on a gameshow: people categorise you, pigeonhole you from three givens, on each of which you can be as truthful as you wish, depending on the extent to which you wish to reinvent yourself: your name; where you come from; the course you are studying. It is most easy to lie about the second.

In the hedonistic atmosphere of a first term at university, I learned little about Shelley or Defoe and lots about why I was professing Welshness to all and sundry. I remember wearing one of those shirts – ubiquitous at the time – emblazoned with an oriental dragon, to Clwb Ifor Bach one night and being accosted by a drunkard with a single question: 'Are you Chinese or Welsh?' Like there was no other option. The answer was easy now, especially after Scott Gibbs went over the line at Wembley, me leaping off the pool table waving a flag around my head, whooping and wailing, baiting the English majority with the rest of the Welsh, to the great surprise of friends down from Brecon who'd seen me do a similar thing when footballer Michael Owen had scored for England against Argentina less than a year earlier.

So what, why, how? When, where, why was this nationality transplant taking place? In those heady university years I was constantly confronted with howls of outrage against my choosing a national identity like I chose what music I listen to or what books to read or what clothes to wear or what breakfast cereal to buy. I realise how hollow it sounds. A cynical manoeuvre: becoming Welsh in 1999.

Nationality is not something you buy into, chop and change, choose because you like it. It's a curse or a blessing. A given. Like your gender or the colour of your skin, it's not something to be messed about with. But I did not become Welsh in Cardiff in 1999. I discovered I am Welsh, had been all along. My main line of defence – against the understandably confused from all over the British Isles – in those frequent interrogations about my Cymric credentials was that I arrived in Wales the week after my third birthday and had spent virtually every day of the intervening two decades here. In official speak, I am Welsh By Residence. But this is not why I once had a St David's cross hanging on my wall or why the words of the anthem send a shiver down my spine or why I care what they mean or why, at first sort of guiltily but more lately proudly, I have voted for Plaid Cymru.

I am not a natural nationalist, and recognise the huge problems nationalisms have caused all over the world. I remember reading a

4

poem by Patrick Jones beginning 'You Sinn Fein fascist, Serb sadist, Welsh nationalist', which made me regret voting Plaid, mun, and being damned (as another Welsh poet had advised). But for a short period at university, all the confused anger that comes with being young, intelligent and uninformed became distilled in the question of national identity. I realised – as soon as I heard them – that I hated English attitudes towards Wales: disdain, ignorance, mild indifference or a patronising love of a valleys accent. I hated them all equally.

I have always held strong views on the important issues of life. I sometimes change my views and sometimes the issues themselves, but whatever views I have, I hold them strongly at the time. So I could not quite believe, or accept, that supposedly educated, supposedly intelligent individuals had come to university with no intention of broadening their minds, their horizons or their experience. There were people enrolled to study sciences with no interest whatsoever in the world around them; literature students with no interest in books; law students with no interest in politics... the list went on. And for some reason, all of these people, at least the ones I came into contact with, came from England. Correction: middle class, Middle England.

On the other hand – and there is obviously a large degree of arbitrariness to all of this and many subsequent exceptions to prove the rule – the Welsh students I met were like me. They were at university to get wasted too, but also they never slept in for lectures. They appreciated the fact they were enjoying a privilege afforded to the very few in our country. Many, like me, craved new experiences and loved having their assumptions challenged. Many, like me, were the first in their family to go to university. And I, like them, and unlike those from 'Middle' England (which is actually the south-east) did not think I came from the natural centre of the civilised world. We realised we came from a small, dark, damp corner of a small island on the edge of the Atlantic.

I found I shared a heritage; that I did belong; that I was Welsh after all. And Cardiff, with its newfound sense of pride and confidence, its architectural rejuvenation, its cultural renaissance and new political importance encapsulated everything I was feeling. And soon, of course, the city became familiar, its buildings and streets and sights and sounds and smells entwined with my life: the puddles of beer on the dancefloor at Metros; the five o'clock in the morning pigeons after a night shift at Queen Street's Burger King; the *Big Issue* sellers; the slow colouring of leaves along Ninian Road; the dust on the shelves in Albany Books; Clarks' pie and chips from XL Fish Bar; the hospital ward up in the Heath where my son was born; his first steps across the living-room of an upstairs flat in Monthermer Road; feeding the swans together at Roath Park; sitting on the bus to Whitchurch next to the kids I was teaching; the chill wind across the river; the filthy language in the pubs and on the street; the roar from the Grange End; the incessant rain; the tears and the laughter; the bad times and the good.

And nowadays this is my city. It's yours too, and everyone's and no one's, because all great cities are, and although this is not a great city, it's a good city and although it's not in my blood, it's in my heart.

Driving Home Both Ways

A470, 2006

I try dropping down a gear, but it's no use. The exhaust is making a terrible racket and the patrol car has already pulled lazily out of its position in a lay-by. The police don't have anything better to do around here. I pull in slowly to the roadside, wind the window down and wait for the inevitable.

'That exhaust doesn't sound too clever.'

I nod.

'Just rev it for me a minute.'

I rev.

'I'm going to have to issue a ticket, I'm afraid.'

He asks where I'm from and I tell him Cardiff.

'And where are you going?'

'Home,' I say, wishing I were already there.

The policeman shoots me a confused glance. 'But you're going the wrong way.'

'Well, I'm from Brecon originally. Home is both ways.'

I first travelled the A470 regularly as a teenager on the old 509 National Express coach between Brecon and Cardiff, and even then grew intensely aware of the extraordinary symbolism with which the road is charged. Even on that short journey, the road passes through three distinctly different worlds. The fare was subsidised to allow these worlds to connect, and I was grateful that three pounds could buy me a complete course in geography, history and sociology; from deceptive rural idyll through post-industrial decline to cosmopolitan capital city in a shade over an hour's coach travel.

And now, of course, I travel the other way; out along Manor Way, where I picked up a speeding fine testing my uncle's theory about the traffic lights; under the bridge which marks the end of Cardiff and the beginning of interminable roadworks and onwards into the inevitable drizzle driving down across the mountains.

That's the great thing about roads: they take you places. Heading north into the mountains, I turn off the roundabout where the A465 Heads of the Valleys intersects with the A470. A couple of gear changes, a steep ascent, a different world.

As sudden and striking as something from children's literature, the experience matches anything from Alice falling down the rabbit hole to Lucy finding a snow-covered forest at the back of her uncle's wardrobe to that young upstart Potter pushing a trolley at a brick wall.

I'm driving home for Christmas and the tops of the mountains are covered in snow; the sky is clear and blue. I check the mirror. My son is sleeping in the back of the car. Belle and Sebastian's *The Boy With the Arab Strap* plays on the stereo. Two weeks' holiday ahead. But then I always feel like this on this road. My road home – both ways.

The A470 is a myth Wales needs, but it's not even a real road. Neatly connecting the truly disparate north and south – 180 miles from Cardiff to Llandudno – and tying up some loose ends on the way, like a dot-to-dot of national identity, the route actually comprises the roads formerly known as the A438, A4073, A479, A44, A492, A489, A4084, A458, A487 and A496. No wonder it's such a drag actually driving the thing.

Wales needs to tell itself the road is real. Welsh Government is spending a fortune improving sections of it; the literature promotion agency had a magazine named after it; artists and photographers have been commissioned to document it; there was a drama series on S4C. And yet I'd be willing to wager that nobody actually travels the entire length of the road for reasons other than perpetuating the myth. There was even an installation at the Wales Millennium Centre – the route's new official starting point – that allowed visitors to 'travel' the road, forwards and backwards at high speed, via digital images. This is clearly a myth someone somewhere wants us to believe in.

Personally, I feel a little cheated by all this engineered cultural mythology, simply because the road is *my* road. The original A470 only went as far as Brecon, which is fine by me because that's the only stretch I drive regularly. For me, the A470 is the road home, both ways. I can't escape it.

After all, if your parents still live in the house where you were brought up, when, if ever, does that really cease to be your home? As much as I feel at home among the binbags and flyposters and curry houses of Cardiff, nothing can match the sense of wellbeing induced by snaking around the bends beneath the Beacons, that first glimpse of the green fields of Mid Wales. There's as strong a sense of homecoming turning off the A40 by the Old Ford in Llanhamlach as there is waiting for the lights to change by Cathays Library. And in spite of all my iconoclastic ranting, I probably love the road – love the myth – more than anyone. If Route 66 is 'The Mother Road', then – at least in my mind – the A470 is the Daddy.

Like most capitals, Cardiff has an uneasy relationship with the rest of the country. People from outside come into the city for work, for shopping, for football and rugby, and then go home again – to a different world. People from inside the city hardly ever go out. And when they do, it's the M4 they go out on, not this road.

The A470 races through the industrial valleys, a dual-carriageway as far as Merthyr. The road gives a great vantage point from which to consider the town's past, present and future: a panoramic vista of remarkable natural location rendered ugly by the brute force of the industrial revolution, a conglomeration of grey houses clinging to the valley sides like lumps of porridge to the edge of an unwashed bowl. In the foreground, a brand new retail park replete with sparkling golden arches and smiling Colonel Sanders. Looming large in the background, the bleak grey stone of Cyfarthfa, the ironmasters' castle, now a museum and a school. The clash of past and present, industrial and post-industrial, closing factories and opening superstores: a lesson in the relentless march of global capitalism and the people who are its perennial losers.

Growing up in Mid Wales, I used to take it as a sign of our backwardness: our nearest McDonalds fifty miles away, a sign that we lived only on the fringes of Western civilisation. Now it's eighteen miles, I'm getting worried.

But thankfully the A470 is not Route 66, punctuated by roadside diners and gas stations. Instead the lay-bys are peppered with hot dog vans, breakfast vans, burger vans, and, in summer, ice-cream vans. Rain or shine and at all times of the day, *y ddraig goch* will be fluttering over Fern's Kitchen, on the edge of the Llwyn Onn reservoir. And the squares of cardboard nailed to the trees near Libanus offering 'Free Tea's and Coffee's for lorry drivers' may infuriate English teachers, but they won't disappoint thirsty road-hauliers.

In the absence of village shops and village pubs, these places are the focal points for communities. Far from being sad, lonely, transitory places for people passing through, there are always a couple of Dai-capped farmers putting the world to rights with the regular lorry drivers over a cuppa and a bacon roll.

There was a time before I'd driven the whole road. I would have, if I hadn't been with friends, insisted on driving into Llandudno town centre and looking up at the Great Orme – journey's end – rather than spending a weekend in Snowdonia. But now I know the middle and northern sections almost as well as the road home: the sharp bend in Builth Wells where the road crosses the river Wye beneath a giant mural of Llewelyn *ein llyw olaf*, the last real Prince of Wales; the concrete towers of the Trawsfynydd nuclear power station; the slate quarries of Blaenau Ffestiniog and the wooded glades of Betws-y-Coed.

I don't care if the road takes no fewer than five turns off the main carriageway, clearly becoming other roads that used to have other numbers and therefore completely debunking the myth. It is, literally and metaphorically, a journey through the heart of Wales. And for me, the road is like an umbilical cord; the comforting thought that my childhood home is always a shade under an hour's drive away. At times of personal crisis, driving the southern stretch of the A470 – the original road – feels like crawling back into the womb, an escape into a safer, less complicated world comprising only earth and sky and a twisting thread of tarmac. And then there's the exhilaration of travelling in the other direction: back towards the city, the present, the real world.

Sometimes it feels not so much like I'm driving home both ways, but like the road itself is my home. I would love to drive and never arrive. The expectation of arrival... no, the forgetting you're anywhere at all: that's the best feeling in the world.

Night falls over Merthyr, a constellation of streetlamps glowing orange in the darkness. It's a Sunday night and the retail park is empty. Beck's *Mutations* plays softly on the stereo. I check the mirror: my son is sleeping. I signal to turn off the roundabout, shift the gears, and head toward the city.

Concrete, steel & sky

Cardiff, 2006

The Millennium Stadium doesn't dominate the Cardiff skyline; it is the Cardiff skyline. After it was completed, they hurriedly started erecting tall buildings around it, just so that it wouldn't look quite so out of place. They failed, of course.

It isn't the most practical location for Europe's largest state-of-the-art retractable roofed sporting arena. Nobody builds giant stadia in a city centre. On matchdays, traffic comes to a halt, roads are closed, buses rerouted. Practically speaking, the idea of a new stadium being built right in the centre of a medium-sized British city, on a riverbank, is absurd. But the Millennium Stadium was never meant to be practical; it wasn't even affordable. Like the baseball field in the Kevin Costner movie, it was built on dreams.

And now, if you look at the cityscape from atop Caerphilly mountain, or from Rover Way bridge, or from Penarth Road or the backstreets of Riverside, it's there. Take in the view from the tower of the castle's Norman keep, or from one of the city's brave new skyscrapers – just how tall does a building have to be before you can call it a skyscraper? – and it's there. It is the skyline; it is the cityscape; it is the sky.

In what seems like the twinkling of an eye, the stadium has come to represent the city itself. It is truly iconic. Trying to imagine Cardiff without the Millennium Stadium is like imagining Paris without the Eiffel Tower, Sydney without the Opera House or Rio without Christ the Redeemer. In the international language of signing, Cardiff is an upturned hand, fingers stretching upward to mimic the stadium's structure. To someone who's never been to the city or to the many thousands who've had their sporting dreams broken and made in the Arms Park cauldron, the Millennium Stadium *is* Cardiff.

A stadium memory:

It was one of those great *where were you when* moments. Where were you when, in the dying minutes of extra time, in front of a passionate 'home' crowd in the team's own city, unloved substitute Andy Campbell replaced cult hero Robert Earnshaw and promptly volleyed Cardiff City back into the upper echelons of British football for the first time in thirty years? Well, actually, I was in the Maesllwch Arms in Glasbury-on-Wye, on my way back from seeing Don DeLillo at Hay Festival.

I'd booked the ticket months in advance, with Cardiff top of the old Division Two, Earnie knocking seven bells out of all-comers and the Bluebirds dead certs for promotion. I had my question ready and everything, about one of those other – more serious – *where were you when* moments: 9/11. I'd wanted to ask DeLillo about where he'd been and what he'd been thinking on that fateful day, seeing as amid the shock and horror I'd been thinking that the whole thing was like something out of a Don DeLillo novel. But with the great man onstage in a packed marquee in Hay-on-Wye, all I could think about was whether Graham Kavanagh had won the toss.

After the talk I jumped in the car and raced to the Maesllwch to catch the second half. Fortunately, the match itself was quite a dull affair, and it was still nil-nil. Extra time and the rest is history. For my part, I caused enough of a scene in a quiet Mid Wales pub on a Sunday afternoon when the goal went in for the woman behind the bar to comment.

'You should have been there,' she said.

I thought of DeLillo, the ex-recluse, ambling through *Cosmopolis*.

'Yes,' I said, 'I should.'

It had been a day to remember, apparently. One to tell the grandchildren about. Reports in the *Echo* and the *Western Mail* talked of a sea of blue making the short walk to the stadium from all parts of the city. The aerial shots on Sky TV kept showing the two grounds, emphasising the proximity of the Millennium to Ninian Park. What followed was the capital's biggest impromptu street party. And in years to come, I'll be able to tell my grandchildren: 'Actually, I wasn't there.'

I *was* there amid the delirium when Wales won that famous victory over Italy, and I was there when Russia broke our hearts. I was there too in the stadium's early days, a Rugby World Cup rout against Japan, but I better remember the very first match hosted by the stadium – a rare victory over South Africa – viewed through the window of Dixons on Queen Street, pictures beamed via satellite from less than half a mile away. And I remember feeling, for once, a real part of a Liverpool victory when Michael Owen turned things around against Arsenal in 2001; they'd won the cup because they'd come to my city.

So it is precisely those times when you're not bodily inside the stadium that it's at its most powerful. These are the times, the match on television, away fans parking in your street, eating in your caff and drinking in your pub, helicopters circling outside your window, when you begin to understand something of its potency in the realm of dreams.

And perhaps this is the point. In a postmodern world where we're so used to having our hopes and dreams 'funnelled' through the prism of the mass media, we begin to prefer the second-hand experience to the real thing. We like to feel a part of something, but we also like to watch it on a screen.

Another stadium memory:

Again, I am not there. At least, I am not physically inside the

1.5 million cubic metre capacity 'bowl'. I do not have a ticket. I am not a statistic. I am not one of the 74,500 people who are actually witnessing Wales beating Ireland to achieve their first Grand Slam triumph in my lifetime.

And yet, I am here as much as anyone. I have queued for a pee and added to the moat surrounding City Hall. 'We pay enough council tax, don't we?' reasons a shaven-headed man whom I wouldn't mind betting my place in the queue pays his council tax to Rhondda Cynon Taff, not Cardiff. If at all. But today not even the Lord Mayor himself would quibble. Not on Grand Slam Day. Not while the hopes and dreams of so many people hang heavy in the sky.

I am here on the civic lawn among the red-shirted throng. I can see the people hanging from every available lamppost, flagpole and tree. I can hear the roar every time Wales surge forward, retrieve the ball, score a try, kick into touch. I am contributing to the racket, the bedlam, the pandemonium. But I cannot see the screen. Nobody can. The sun is directly behind it, and most spectators are more intent on singing and drinking than shielding their eyes and watching the game.

But I can see the stadium; concrete, steel and sky.

Together, Stronger

Cardiff, 2016

In the winter of 1925, 100,000 people lined the streets of Cardiff
to witness the cortège of the forty-four-year-old former
featherweight British boxing champion 'Peerless' Jim Driscoll
winding its way toward Cathays Cemetery. Two years later, Cardiff
City Football Club won the FA Cup, taking the trophy out of
England for the first and still the only time. Crowds of 150,000
turned out for the open top bus tour to welcome their heroes
home. Despite slipping out of living memory, both events have
entered the collective imagination of the city.

In an age when dress codes betrayed one's social status, both
events saw bowler hats mingle with flat caps and all classes of men
clamber up the gaslamps for a better view. As such, they capture a
snapshot of a city, united in grief and in celebration, and prove
that Cardiff has always been a place where sport is both a social
leveller and a barometer of collective mood. This summer's
European football championship began before the referendum on
Britain's membership of the EU, and the ensuing political turmoil
that has threatened to tear apart at least one union of nations; it is
easy to remark that Wales' successful campaign, with its attendant
feelgood factor and hashtag of #togetherstronger, has taken the
bite out of Brexit. But as well as being a panacea for political ills,
that which brings us out on the streets perhaps also shows us what
we really care about, where our hearts are.

Such public mass events capture a mood and a moment. Crowds

– as opposed to homogenised masses – are gatherings based on shared emotion. You can physically be there, or – in the age of mass media – participate from where you are. The assassination of President Kennedy is often cited as the first global moment where 'you remembered where you were'; many have followed, the power of television heightening the sense of proximity viewers feel to far-flung events: war in Vietnam; revolution in Iran; the fall of the Berlin Wall; repression in Tiananmen Square; the release from prison of Nelson Mandela; the September 11 attacks on the World Trade Centre. Sociologists, psychologists and cultural critics had a field day in the wake of the death of Diana, Princess of Wales in 1997. Pivotal moments in world history become memorably charged because they play out in our living rooms. We feel closer to events, more involved, than the generations who have preceded us, receiving their news from the wireless, the newspaper, the town crier and word-of-mouth. We watch history unfold in front of our eyes.

But, of course, we don't. We were no more there in Saigon or Tehran, Berlin or Beijing, Cape Town or New York than we are today via Twitter in Fallujah or Benghazi, Brussels or Dallas – or Cardiff Bay. Social media, of course, works both ways; we are creators, as well as consumers, of content. We can add comments to blogs and online news articles. We can feel involved, but we are not – physically – *there*.

And so we continue to crave moments like this. When Aaron Ramsey, the golden-haired golden boy from Caerphilly and quite possibly player of the tournament, appeared on one of the turrets of Cardiff Castle, in a perfect juxtaposition of Wales past and present, he was taking pictures and tweeting about us even as we were taking pictures and tweeting about him. Later in the afternoon, Wales' manager Chris Coleman summed up the special relationship that has developed between this golden generation of Welsh footballers and the fans by pointing at the stands and saying: 'They deserve them – and they deserve them'. It encapsulates the narrative that has developed in the course of this 'special summer': this is a special team backed by special supporters. Feelings of mutuality contained in #togetherstonger have been actualised; out of the internet and into the real world.

As we look back at the photographs and footage of Jim Driscoll's funeral, we glimpse something of another world; almost a century has elapsed and the world has changed almost beyond recognition, but there is something beyond the buildings, the modes of transport, the clothes, the manners, the attitudes, the faces. Everything and nothing has changed. Walking away from the castle, across the bridge over the Taff, past Ivor Novello's blue plaque and out onto Wellington Street toward the Canton and Grangetown districts of the city that have long buttressed the Cardiff City Stadium and its predecessor at Ninian Park, I wonder how history will perceive this generation of Cardiffians.

If we imagine, erroneously, the world of the 1920s in black and white, monochrome photography bequeathing us an unrealistically drab view of the world as it was, it is hard not to see this year's parade in glorious technicolour. Red shirts; green and white flags; yellow bucket hats; blue skies. A route to a football ground that was for decades associated with some of the worst hooliganism, idiotic intimidation, violence and vitriol in the whole of the UK was lined on Friday evening by people from all of Cardiff's communities. A cross-section of ages, races and social backgrounds stood together, united by the flag and the achievements of the team but also by something stronger: a desire to be part of something bigger than ourselves, to bear witness in person not to extraordinary events, but to wave and be waved at by a busload of men in tracksuits, and to take photographs with our mobile phones.

The stadium event itself threatened to gorge itself on obvious, 'iconic' tropes of Welshness. 'Delilah' was rapturously received by a crowd that would, frankly, have sung along to anything by anybody with a Welsh grandmother. But Tom Jones' anthem did jar a little, representing as it does the slightly outmoded 1970s version of Welshness celebrated at rugby internationals; leaving aside its murderous lyrics, it is incongruous in a football context given that it is also a terrace anthem at Stoke City. Other tunes played by the DJ from Capital FM hinted at the rich and varied musical tapestry that comprises the soundtrack to Welsh football history: 'Kernkraft 400' by the Bavarian techno outfit Zombie Nation and Franki Valli's 1967 hit 'Can't Take My Eyes Off You' are as unlikely as bedfellows as they are as football anthems, but between them they manage to conjure up the many failures and sporadic successes of the Welsh football team.

Of the live performers, Kizzy Crawford perhaps best encapsulated something of the contemporary Wales to which the current crop of footballing superstars belong. A Welsh speaker with Bajan heritage, the soul-folk-jazz singer warmed the gathering crowd up gently with her own songs and a lovely medley comprising a wordless 'Men of Harlech', 'Calon Lân' and a playful version of the Euro 2016 fans' favourite 'Ain't Nobody (Like Joe Ledley)'. Crawford is confident, fun-loving, talented – just like the team she welcomed home. At nineteen, she is also of their generation. Mike Peters, the fifty-seven-year-old former lead singer with The Alarm, would seem to represent the opposite end of the spectrum. But his acoustic rock version of 'The Bells of Rhymney' reverberated movingly around the stadium, ensuring a strange but entirely appropriate sense of melancholy underscored an occasion that flirted with but ultimately rejected triumphalism (appropriate because despite the hype this was a proud thank you rather than a winners' parade – lest we forget that Wales lost their semi-final).

Manic Street Preachers were the final support act to the real headliners, the Welsh players. 'We're here for the same reason as all of you,' said James Dean Bradfield, 'to say thank you to our heroes.' It seems that a big event in the life of the nation is not complete without the Manics bellowing out 'A Design for Life'. Manic Millennium; *The Passion of Port Talbot*; even the opening of the Welsh Assembly is better remembered for the band's refusal to play in front of the Queen than for the artists who accepted the invitation to the gala concert. And despite the forced lyrics to 'Together Stronger (C'mon Wales)', the band's attempt to play Skinner, Baddiel and the Lightning Seeds to Wales' England of Euro 96, when they sing 'So come on Ramsey, let's set the world alight / When Gareth Bale plays, we can beat any side', it feels slightly less queasy because it actually happened. Chris Coleman invited us to dream; we did, and for one summer only the dream came true.

So as the players took their final lap of honour in the Cardiff sunshine, and the mutual appreciation reached fever pitch, somehow the First Minister waiting on the tarmac at Cardiff Airport, a guided walk around Cardiff Castle and an open top bus tour of the city centre, a circling helicopter and 200,000 people lining the streets did not seem like an 'over the top' homecoming for beaten semi-finalists. For most people, this was not about winning or losing, it was truly about taking part. And as we thronged the streets our smiles spoke volumes about who we are and what we value as a nation. Future historians may yet judge us badly for what could turn out to be skewed priorities – cheering footballers while the political world imploded – but we'll always have the memories, and besides, there are far worse ways of asserting your nationhood than dreaming dreams, acting in a spirit of togetherness, and, of course, singing songs. Do take me home.

What They Were About,
We Are About

Newport, 2017

The six points of the People's Charter (for which thousands fought and for which, in Newport, over twenty died) have all long since been accepted as cornerstones of representative democracy: universal suffrage; the secret ballot; equal constituencies; payment for members of parliament and the absence of a 'property qualification'. We don't have annual parliaments, as the Charter demanded, but we do have fixed terms. In the long run, the people won. John Frost, former mayor and the main leader of the Newport revolt, who had his death sentence transmuted to transportation to Australia, returned a hometown hero. He was given an unconditional pardon in 1856 and was free to continue his reformist organising and writing until his death at the age of ninety-three.

But fast-forward to our own young century and the story is not so clear. Two years ago, Manic Street Preachers, from the former Chartist stronghold of Blackwood, wrote a song called 'The View from Stow Hill'. Stow Hill is the name of one of the oldest streets in Newport. It gives its name to the electoral ward that covers most of the city centre. According to legend, St Gwynllyw was the earliest resident of Stow Hill. St Woolos, Newport's cathedral, is named after him, albeit in a very strange anglicisation. Stow Hill also marked the final stage of the Chartists' journey to the Westgate Hotel, where they were faced with gunfire when they tried to storm the hotel to free their comrades on the morning of November 4, 1839. Around twenty-two were killed.

A walk down Stow Hill today cuts to the quick. The Westgate Hotel now houses Poundworld, a closed down shop that used to sell vape liquids and a closed down branch of Starbucks. It faces a giant branch of Sports Direct, infamous for its use of zero hours contracts, outside which the city's homeless pitch their tents and hawk the *Big Issue*. The scene of the 1839 carnage is at the very heart of Wales' third biggest city, and yet what Nicky Wire's lyric observes is physical and spiritual degradation. 'Casual litter' and 'pitiful nihilism'. Empty shops, pound shops, charity shops. On the surface, it is difficult to see Newport as the global symbol of freedom and democracy that it could, perhaps should, one day become. 'Cheapness surrounds me,' sings James Dean Bradfield, 'but I'm not looking.'

Just as the industrialisation of the Gwent valleys fuelled the misery of injustice that was to foment a hotbed of radicalism in the nineteenth century, the ravages of the late twentieth-century's de-industrialisation are still here for all to see: a fallout of poverty, addiction, petty crime, unemployment and hopelessness.

But if we 'look up to the skies' as 'The View from Stow Hill' urges, we can – just about – sense 'a little hope'. As you walk down Stow Hill today, don't look at the litter, don't be tempted by nihilism. There is a point and a purpose to your steps. The footsteps you follow belong to those who believed in better. The burning flame of hope that inspired the martyrs who were crushed all those scores of Novembers ago can be rekindled for our own time.

Today, as we march down Stow Hill, from St Woolos Cathedral at the top to Westgate Square at the bottom, it will be an act of commemoration; we will remember those who died, who gave their lives for a noble cause. It will be an act of celebration too, because there is no doubt that we have more freedom, better living and working conditions and more effective political representation than those who went before us. But there is also a necessity that today's march is an exploration. We need to ask ourselves: are we fit to walk in their footsteps? Are their boots too big for us? Or can we grow into them as we get into our stride?

We may have the vote, but do we use it? And how? And are we content to blithely celebrate British democracy while all around the world our fellow men and women – particularly women – continue to be denied that basic right? We may have the privilege of a polling booth and a ballot box, but what about the many countries around the world where elections are nothing more than an elaborate sham?

177 years ago, we lost twenty-two. In the Democratic Republic of Congo, forty-four were killed in election protests last September. At least fifty-two people were shot at an anti-government protest during a religious festival in Ethiopia in October. The ongoing war in Syria began with the regime's crackdown on pro-democracy protests. Wherever you look, the fight for freedom goes on – and today Newport footsteps echo around the world.

We must also question British democracy. In terms of numbers of electors, we have equal constituencies. Gone are the days of 'rotten boroughs' – but do we really believe that today's shifting electoral boundaries are free from gerrymandering? Equally, it is a little ironic to think now of the working classes of the 1830s taking to the streets to demand MPs be paid. They wanted working men to be able to enter parliament; post expenses scandal and in an age where politicians earn three times the average salary, one wonders what kind of demands about politicians' paypackets might make it onto a People's Charter today.

As you walk Stow Hill, notice the churches feeding the homeless and welcoming refugees; notice the volunteer Samaritans inhabiting the darkest hours of the lives of strangers; notice the aptly named Share Centre and its array of classes, activities and events; notice the friendly banter across the road between the Red

Lion and the Baneswell Social Club; notice the solicitors fighting for justice on behalf of their clients and the watchmakers plying their expert trade.

This is Newport now. Almost a half-century after *les evenements* in Paris in May 1968, when the protest slogan was *Sous les paves, la plage* – 'Under the paving stones, the beach', we are still searching for the beach of freedom and justice under the paving stones of oppression. The artworks comprising *In Their Footsteps* are cast and carved in ceramic and stone, but their legacy needs to be enacted in flesh and blood. Real feet in real boots on real pavements demanding real change.

Imagined Communities

Bilbao, 2013

The first thing it did was rain. As the long-distance grey and blue ALSA bus pulled into and then out of the red and grey city of Bilbao, up into the hills of the Basque country, it began to drizzle in such a way as to make the grey and the green settle in my mind as well as on the window of the coach. I recognised the feeling, as well as the weather, straight away. After months of unending Mediterranean sunshine in my new home on the arid east coast of Spain, the Basque rain provoked a deep and immediate *hiraeth*. It was not only a longing for home, but a confirmation that, wherever I go in the world, and for however long, Wales will always be that home. I suppose I am telling you this personal story because perhaps it confirms, at least in my mind, the very existence of something called a nation.

According to theory, Wales and the Basque Country are both examples of 'assimilated peripheral nations'. They share the very loose definition of being formed from 'a community of people who share a common language, culture, ethnicity, descent or history' without a general recognition of the 'much more impersonal, abstract and overtly political' definition of a Nation State; that is, 'a cultural-political community that has become conscious of its coherence, unity and particular interests'. Each nation, to varying degrees, has had its nationalists, those who would argue strongly that in both places there is a strong case for 'geographical collision', that the cultural nation deserves a political recognition. And both have achieved a greater degree of political recognition and autonomy in the last thirty years.

Some of the parallels between Wales and the Basque country are well documented, the Basques having become something of a *cause célèbre* for aspiring nationalists in all small European nations. Even the most cursory resumé of national statistics reveals some startling similarities. Wales is a country of 8,022 square miles, with a population of three million. The Basque Country is a region of 8,088 square miles with a population of three million. If I described a primarily agrarian country whose towns and cities nevertheless rapidly expanded through in-migration to host heavy industries that served the purposes of the wider state beyond its borders, you would be right in guessing at either. Likewise if I were to explain how post-industrial decline has led to the rise of service industries and cultural tourism, or how the principal cities have undergone large-scale regeneration projects centred on iconic buildings, or if I talked about the importance of sport in forging and expressing a cultural identity, or how the countryside is still characterised by a timeless combination of small market towns and scattered farmhouses.

The two countries are to a large extent defined by the continuing stubborn existence of their respective minority languages, each of which has survived against the odds, each protected to some degree by the mountainous landscape of the homeland. Here Euskera and Cymraeg took refuge as the territories associated with their speakers were subsumed by dominant neighbours in the process of becoming imperial world powers. And just as Cymru is 'The land of the Cymry', *Herri* in Euskera means a country, a nation, a people or settlement; therefore the native term *Euskal Herria* for what the Spanish call 'El Pais Vasco', which in English we call 'The Basque Country', is a useful clue in understanding Basque self-perception. 'Country of Basque Speakers' foregrounds the language to such an extent that we are forced to consider whether that, above all else perhaps, is what a nation might be: a linguistic grouping. It's a difficult proposition to make in a country where only 19% of the population speak Cymraeg, but is made doubly interesting by the fact that only 27% of the population of 'Euskal Herria' currently speak Euskera, and that despite, in the post-Franco years at least, much of the social engineering we would recognise here.

The dominant Basque landscapes are dramatic coastlines and endless green mountains. Walking the *Norte* – the rugged northern route of the Camino de Santiago – I was perpetually struck by sights that reminded me of home. The low-key surf town of Zarautz put me in mind of Solva, Calle San Francisco in downtown Bilbao made me think of Grangetown, and somewhat strangely, and movingly, Guernica reminded me of Machynlleth. Maybe, especially after that emotional arrival, where the ALSA bus out of Bilbao made me recall the exact feeling I used to get on the National Express out of Cardiff – past Castell Coch and out into the hinterlands of Rhondda Cynon Taf and Merthyr – I was looking for it. There has even been research to suggest these two tribes, occupying actually very different mountain nations on Western Europe's wet Atlantic Fringe, are – despite Euskera's famous status as a non Indo-European 'language isolate' – *genetically* linked.

However, as tempting as it is to see only the parallels the differences are striking too. As noticeable as the Cambrian-esque landscape of Euskal Herria are the manner of nationalist sentiments. 'Tourist: You are neither in Spain nor France. You are in the Basque Country,' announces a banner in the heart of Donostia/San Sebastian's old town. It is an unnecessary assertion. A visitor to Gipuzkoa, one of the Spanish Autonomous Community of the Basque Country's three constituent regions, could hardly fail to notice the banners depicting a united Euskadi, stretching across the France-Spain border, in silhouette, together with nationalist slogans, that hang like washing from every other apartment. In neighbouring Vizcaya, as well as the red-and-white stripes of Athletic Club Bilbao replacing the blue-and-white of San Sebastian's Real Sociedad, there is also a wider preference for the *ikurriña* – the Basque national flag. Here, despite the flag's red, white and green livery (yet another reminder of Wales), politics is a way of life in a way far more comparable to the North of Ireland.

The history of the Basques, as the very name of its ancient capital – Gernika in its native orthography – and the simple three-letter acronym ETA (Euskadi Ta Askatasuna – Basque Homeland and Freedom) attest, is one of violent, bloody struggle. Under Franco, like other 'regionalist' flags – that of Catalunya, for example – the *ikurriña* was outlawed. The blood that R.S. Thomas saw as going into 'the making of the wild sky' in Wales is here not consigned to the 'past', 'sham ghosts', 'quarries and mines'. The last serious armed national liberation struggle does not date to a time of cattle rustling and castle razing; it is very much in living memory, the final ETA ceasefire announcement coming in 2011. Even now, in the tentative peace that exists, there are very public campaigns to repatriate the political prisoners of the bloody conflict.

Modern European nationalisms were a result of, and reaction to, the late nineteenth-century's fortification of the nation state as the world's primary, and later only, way of organising its territories. In the Basque Country, and Wales, as elsewhere, there were revivals in questions of nationality that laid the ground for the course each nation was to take in the twentieth-century and beyond. A comparison of the trajectories of nationalism in each country allows us to see the very idea of a nation; and, depending on your point of view, a nation is *nothing if not*, or *nothing but*, an idea.

Nations are constructed identities. Sometimes they coincide with geography or language or ethnicity, but none of these are a precondition. In Cymru and in Euskal Herria, the landscapes may be similar and the languages may have endured a parallel battle to survive but much of the insignia, regalia and quasi-national paraphernalia associated with each country today is the product of the last 150 years of sometimes slow and haphazard, but nevertheless deliberate, nation building.

Let's take the Basque example. The *ikurriña*, which has come to be recognised as the national flag, was originally designed in 1894 by Luis and Sabino Arana, founders of the Basque National Party, the EAJ-PNV. It depicts the red earth of Vizcaya overlaid with a green saltire representing the oak of Guernica (the tree which represents the ancient *fueros* or laws) and the white cross of the Catholic Church. Its original association with a single wing of opinion within the region meant it wasn't until 1938 and Franco's prohibition of the flag that it became a powerful symbol of defiance (used frequently by ETA and only recognised officially in 1977). The heraldic symbol of the Basque Country is the *Zazpiak Bat* ('The seven are one'). It is a coat of arms that depicts all seven of the regions (Vizcaya, Gipuzkoa and Alava, plus Navarre in Spain, and Labourd, Soule and Lower Navarre in France). It was designed in 1897. During this period, ideas of the territorial integrity of a Basque 'nation' spanning the existing political borders was developed, and it was through emblematic representation that this ideal was best expressed.

The contemporary prevalence of silhouetted maps of this integral territory further underscores the power of pictorial representation to create ideas of nationhood in the minds of the populace. Indeed, Professor Steven Weber of the University of Berkeley, California, has posited the theory that the idea of the nation state was prefigured by fifteenth-century developments in mapmaking technology; certainly the issue of a country's border has been at the forefront of politics and war for at least the last half-millennium. It might be tempting therefore to see the antiquity of Offa's Dyke – an eighth-century construction – as a pleasing piece of evidence of Wales' territorial continuity, relative to the chequered and somewhat lesser-known history of the Euskera-speaking peoples. But one might need only look to evidence as recent as the Local Government Act 1972, which finally settled centuries of ambiguity of the status of

Monmouthshire within Wales, or indeed to a Wales that includes or has included, in addition to the many official changes in local administration, popularly recognised regions such as 'Y Fro', 'The Valleys', 'The Marches', 'Border Country' and 'Little England Beyond Wales'. Like the Basque Country, Wales is not linguistically or culturally homogenous. Surveys like the one conducted in the province of Navarre, finding that 71% of respondents did not define themselves as Basque and 53% opposed measures to support Euskera as a language, sound familiar even if the figures do not tally exactly with perspectives in, say for example, Flintshire or Brecknock.

The lesson of history is therefore that, far from being what it purports to be – a fixed point or common thread – the idea of a nation is a fluid and malleable one. At times, it hardens into a fixity; these are perhaps the occasions when nationalism's negative connotations come to the fore. But at other times – times perhaps like this – where the idea of the nation softens, when the guns have fallen silent and a *conversation* begins, we have the chance to reaffirm and rediscover, revive or reinvent aspects of the family myth that have been a help or a hindrance in the past. In 1983, the theorist Benedict Anderson wrote of nations that they are 'imagined communities'. And so as I stepped off the coach and onto Basque soil for the first time, perhaps appropriately in the town of Irun – at the border locals refuse to recognise – I decided to keep reminding myself: the parallels with Wales are fancies I am imposing upon the place. It is not like Wales, not really. But everywhere I looked, in the dappled sunlight of forest glades and in the misty mornings and quiet harbours, and in the bustling market towns and green, green hills, the landscape told a different story. Even surrounded by the unfamiliar trappings of über-nationalism, everywhere banners and flags and graffito slogans, I find myself caught up in a self-conscious Romantic idealism, daydreaming about the kind of country I would like, trying to imagine a community.

Things and People of Obaba

Obaba, 2013

Obaba is a small, remote village in the heart of the Basque Country, full of characters and full of character. If you haven't read, or at least heard about, Bernardo Atxaga's prize-winning, genre-defying 'short story collection' *Obabakoak*, you would not know that in describing Obaba thus I am engaging in a kind of literary game, the kind the author himself plays with readers of his book. Obaba, you see, is only a village as much as Llareggub is a village; it exists in the mind of its creator, and has therefore enjoyed an ongoing life – or series of lives – in the minds of the readers of perhaps the most celebrated Basque language work ever committed to paper. Atxaga (1951-) is well aware of the absurd situation in which he finds himself, as the 'Shakespeare of Euskera'. Being the leading writer of the generation that came of age in the years when the arrival of democracy in Spain meant Basques could write in their own tongue, Atxaga found himself having to (re)invent Euskera as a literary language.

Before *Obabakoak* appeared in 1988, to international acclaim, an estimated total of just four hundred books had been published in Basque since the early sixteenth-century. For me, this exceptionality alone means Obaba deserves its place alongside the West Wales setting of *Under Milk Wood* and Gabriel Garcia Marquez's Macondo as one of literature's great fictional locations – and not only in the sense that it is a 'made-up place'. Unlike the aforementioned places, which have supposed real-world

31

counterparts in New Quay or Laugharne, and Aracataca, Colombia, you will not find even an equivalent of Obaba on a map. Atxaga's skill has been to make Obaba the centre-point of an entire literary universe. Its title means simply 'Things and people of Obaba'. If anything, he has created a Basque Everyplace, within which no one can be an Everyman.

Where that most celebrated of short story collections, James Joyce's *Dubliners*, made a fictionalised version of the writer's native city, Obaba is like the capital of Atxaga's imagination. It contains infinities. My use of inverted commas around 'short story collection' is entirely deliberate. *Obabakoak* is a postmodern yet direct descendant of *Dubliners*, but also stretches its intertextuality across folktales and fairytales, literary theory and the modern short story. As well as being genre-defying, it is thought-provoking and utterly beguiling.

First and perhaps foremost, it is a writer's book. Atxaga is a writer's writer in the manner of Borges or Kundera, full of linguistic and literary trickery. The book begins with a writer, surrounded by books and by writing. The first section, 'Childhoods', is the most obvious descendant of the Joycean idea of tracing a life through lives, beginning at beginnings. In the second section, 'Nine Words in Honour of the Village of Villamediana', which is both a self-contained collection of interlinked short stories and connected through various means to the rest of the book, the local literati discuss the very nature of storytelling. Their story is intertwined with their stories, their fictional lives linked to their fiction. But the non-existence of Obaba is not merely the postmodernist trick you might expect it to be; it is a world in the best sense of the word. It is, to use the phrase Benedict Anderson uses to describe 'real' nations, an 'imagined community'. As a writer, and as a reader, it grows to become a world you long to be part of.

I often found myself in that rare, delicious wallowing state, infused with a sense of being buried deep inside layers of stories.

Populated by characters who are themselves storytellers, in Obaba Atxaga creates a world that is akin to the idea of a dream within a dream. It gives rise to the thought that communities who place games at their very heart are those for whom it is clearest that life itself is, in many ways, a game. Not for one moment do I mean that life is not also, absolutely, deadly serious. The final sentence of *Obabakoak* captures perfectly the position and circumstances of Obaba's composition. Acknowledging the fears of 'prison' and 'skull' and 'a sinister man dressed in green and wearing a top hat', all squares in a mysterious board game called The Game of the Goose, Atxaga promises to 'keep writing': 'the reason the board is there is for us to continue playing'.

The board, you are left to feel, is both the book and the world. Atxaga's epilogue is entitled 'By way of an autobiography'. It is here he claims 'a particular view of life... a description of the tasks and the days we are allotted on this earth', a game of both 'Chance' and 'Free Will', 'a journey full of difficulties'. It is with this analogy that Atxaga himself (but not, perhaps, the man behind the nom-de-plume, Joseba Irazu Garmendia) steps out from behind the curtain. And it is here that he defines himself in reference to his country. Atxaga is, in his own words, 'a Basque writer born in 1951'. Without a choice and through no fault of his own therefore, he is also a writer of exceptional circumstance; that he happens also to be a writer of exceptional talent has only added to the self-conscious burden that he carries. 'By the time [I] was twenty-three', the 'Shakespeare of Euskera' confides, 'I had read all of the Basque literature that the dictator had not managed to burn.'

Obabakoak was born of the possibly unique situation of its writer's having read everything in the language in which it was written, but also of his having supplemented the lack of national antecedents with a thorough grounding in fiction from across the continents and centuries. Tellingly, Atxaga's epilogue namechecks *The Arabian Nights*, *Moby Dick* and Kafka's *Metamorphosis* as examples of works now available 'in shops, in libraries, everywhere'.

All three can be perceived as influences on the literary hall-of-mirrors that is *Obabakoak*. But where Atxaga's autobiographical postscript really captures something of the late twentieth-century zeitgeist is in its insistence that:

> These days nothing can be said to be peculiar to one place or one person. The world is everywhere and Euskal Herria is no longer just Euskal Herria but – as Celso Emilio Ferreiro would have said – 'the place where the world takes the name Euskal Herria'.

This simple phrase hints also of something hopeful for our own, twenty-first, century: a chance for progressive nationalisms based not on misplaced pride or blind prejudice, but on careful consideration of language and culture and for literature that is specific to a place but speaks to the world by reaching out, like all good stories do, across continents and centuries and invented boundaries.

A Fiesta in Every Town

Deba, 2013

There is something about somebody else's village fête that encourages romanticism. Quite apart from the exoticism inherent in observing the customs of others, there is a universal turning-of-the-seasons melancholy to a festival that is effortlessly inclusive of all age groups. Sitting in the afternoon sunlight watching the young people of Deba enjoying their *corrida* could not fail to make one lament the transient nature of youth; at dusk, watching more elderly denizens slow-dance to the jauntiness of the *trikitixa* (the Basque diatonic accordion), this lamentation becomes one for the transient nature of life. Even at the height of summer, there is an autumnal quality to the fading light.

No people on earth parties quite like the Spanish, and although the people of Deba would be the first to tell you they are Basque not Spanish, they have in common with their neighbours in Aragon and Castile and Andalusia an ability to celebrate every occasion as if it might well be the last. The shops close all day, the bars are open all night. There is no escape from the madness, even if you want it, and nobody does. 'This is the fishermen's day,' explains a local schoolgirl, dressed, like all of her peers, in long blue skirt, white blouse and the checked neckerchief *de rigeur* with both sexes and all age groups. It is not a national costume or a national day; this is simply one more festival.

In Donostia/San Sebastian, we planned our passing through to coincide with La Semana Grande – the Big Week of music and dancing whose highlight is a nightly fireworks display over the bay of La Concha. We spent half the night dancing on the edge of the beach. Against a backdrop of hyper-traditional parades that felt like a cross between an Eisteddfod and a revolution, the beachside DJ played hip-hop, trip-hop and cutting-edge mixes of Brazilian rumbas. If that was not what we expected, it also came as a surprise that as we tramped across the *montes Vascos* on the Camino de Santiago, there seemed to be a fiesta in *every* town.

In Zumaia, the roads were closed off to allow a hillside go-karting race to proceed to the sound of Basque folk-reggae pumping through a tinny tannoy; in Bilbao stages were set up for music and dancing and street theatre, while participants in water-games were watched by thousands lining the banks of the river. Here in Deba, it was all about the bulls. Not the magnificent *toros* of *Death in the Afternoon*, the traditional activity contested by animal rights activists, nor the famous *encierro* of Pamplona during the Fiesta de San Fermin or their fire-based equivalents in San Sebastian. In Deba, the bulls are babies and the derring-do is done by the children of the town; in my continuing quest to find Welsh equivalence to every experience in Euskal Herria, it didn't take me long to recall the welly wanging at Llanfihangel Show.

The heady mixture of music and a-day-out-for-all-the-family doesn't take long to leave me nostalgic for my south Powys childhood of shows and country fairs, events I came to think of as boring as my teenage self began to clamour for the excitement of a city – any city would do. Now I recognise the central importance of these time-honoured rural traditions. However beguiling, beautiful or bonkers a tradition might seem to outsiders, for locals such rituals mark the turning of the years, forming the very punctuation points of life. Having long since been saturated by an urban culture that can only revive such mystical events with a protective coating of irony and faux-nostalgic 'vintage' knowingness, here in the Basque Country I find myself longing not only for home in the sense of a specific place but a certain type of community.

Deba's central square has been converted wholesale into a makeshift bullring, its wooden fences less than a metre from front doors, residents' balconies overnight becoming akin to theatrical boxes while the stalls are formed from long planks of wood fixed up as benches. The audience is predominantly young and the atmosphere reminds me of a school assembly on the day the oldest group of pupils will leave, complete with rowdy chanting, near-universal flirtatiousness and conspicuous evidence of underage alcohol consumption. We join a song of support of the crowd's favourite baby bull avoider, a big-boned Basque girl of fifteen or sixteen with jet-black hair and a wicked smile: 'Sofie, Sofie, lo lo lo lo lo...'

Outside the arena, the bars that would ordinarily line the edges of the square with regiments of chrome-legged chairs and tables spill their punters out onto the street. Bar staff, themselves decked out in the ubiquitous fisherman's garb, are hardly visible behind *pintxos* stacked in formations like Jenga towers on narrow formica counters. In the corner of each, a television blares out the Real Sociedad game, to varying levels of interest. Away from the town centre, there is a fairground, a market and the beach. At seven in the morning, when we're setting out for the next town, revellers are still parading through alleyways. The teenagers have been out all night, following the music.

Travel writing is so often a first-person account. And the idea of travel's capacity to extend one's horizons, expand one's mind and teach one about oneself is so often platitudinous. But I'd like to conclude by wondering: if other people's festivals can make you feel like this much of an outsider, this much of a passer-through not just of a single town but of life itself, imagine how wonderful and strange are the things you regard as normality. Imagine a Six Nations match in Cardiff viewed through the eyes of a Basque fisherman or the National Eisteddfod through the eyes of a Hackney hipster. Maybe we can yet reclaim the idea of tradition from CathKidstonisation.

In Wales, we do not lack a rich seam of folk tradition waiting to be tapped into; we already have contemporary culture, one that blends the best of past and present. But maybe it is only *without* government sanction, corporate sponsorship or, dare I say it, arts council funding, that we can truly discover why customs exist in the first place. La Semana Grande in San Sebastian, Wales v England in Cardiff, the *corrida* in Deba and the welly wanging at Llanfihangel Show are all part of the same thing – the continuity of community. It's up to us all, of course, but if it were left to me to imagine a community, I'd want a fiesta in every town.

The Art of War

Gernika, 2013

Before the destruction of the quiet market town of Gernika, deep in the Basque hills, there had been a similar assault on Durango. The Italians had performed similar atrocities in Abyssinia and their planes were to support the Nazis and their Spanish allies in this campaign to demoralise the Basques. But Gernika (Basque spelling) is forever remembered as the site of the first act of total war: a wilful and deliberate attack on a civilian population who were, despite the atmosphere of intense intimidation fostered by rebel generals Franco and Mola, going about their weekly business.

April 26th 1937 would have been market day, and despite subsequent disputes between historians as to whether a market was actually held on that fateful Monday, it is clear that the timing of the bombing – which lasted three hours – was intended to cause as much death and destruction as possible. Bilbao, along with its Catalan counterpart Barcelona, formed not only the industrial bedrock of Spain, but also the powerbase of support for the democratically elected leftist government in Madrid. The order to attack Gernika was a strategic move, a warning to Bilbao.

It was also an effort to destroy the spiritual home of the Basque nation, and thus an early attempt – even before Franco had seized power – at forging a new idea of Spain. Its Gernikako Arbola – the famous 'Tree of Guernica' – is a symbol of the freedoms of Biscayan people, and by extension all of the Basques. Dating back to the fourteenth-century, the tree forms a link with the days when medieval assemblies were held under large trees, often oaks. This tradition of village democracy could not be further removed from the debut act of total war from the Luftwaffe's Condor Legion.

In attempting to obliterate the town, along with its tree, the rebels who were to become the Francoist dictatorship were striking at the very heart of the Basque nation. In other words, they knew exactly what they were doing, and why. For the Germans, Gernika was a dummy run for the worldwide war that was already looming, where bombing raids on civilian populations would not only become the norm but would grow ever more brutal and disregarding of human life. Gernika paved the way for Coventry and Dresden and Hiroshima. For the Spanish, it was an act of terrorism whose repercussions were to reverberate for the rest of the century.

The attack on Gernika has its status, of course, because of *Guernica* (Spanish spelling) by Pablo Picasso. The painter's masterwork, created for the Spanish Republican Government's pavilion at the 1937 Paris International Exposition is a mural depicting an allegory of the Spanish struggle, which Picasso called 'the fight of reaction against the people, against freedom.' Despite that the Nationalist coup had prompted Picasso's first overtly political works, he went on: 'My whole life as an artist has been nothing more than a continuous struggle against reaction and the death of art... In the panel on which I am working, which I shall call *Guernica*, and in all my recent works of art, I clearly express my abhorrence of the military caste which has sunk Spain in an ocean of pain and death.'

Guernica has become iconic to the point where some of its original impact could have been lost. But its anguished, monochrome figures, twisted out of all proportion, still capture something like the impossible. The mural is an appropriate response to an act that leaves no room for appropriate responses. There are no words to greet such violence. Perhaps this is precisely why Picasso's silent screams retain their power and why it is not simply another painting.

After Paris, the mural travelled to Scandinavia, then London (where it arrived on the day of the 1938 Munich Agreement). Between 1939 and 1952, *Guernica* was hosted by various galleries in the United States, mainly at the Museum of Modern Art in New York. With brief interludes in Brazil and Milan, there it remained until 1981 when it was finally 'repatriated' to Spain, six years after the death of Franco (and eight after Picasso). It now stands as a symbol of resistance – to fascism, to totalitarianism, to senseless, cowardly acts of war – at the Reina Sofia museum in Madrid. Such is the universality it has attained, a replica is hung outside the meeting room of the United Nations Security Council in New York. Picasso's vivid picture made the town of Guernica itself an international symbol of first resistance and later reconciliation. The town now houses a museum and research centre for peace.

The claims of the Franco regime to have had nothing to do with the bombing (both immediately afterwards and for many years to follow) are undermined not only by the facts of the bombing but also by the fact of the place. While war criminals and cultural vandals know how to destroy symbols (sadly, there have been many Gernikas, before and since), they rarely know how to *create*. Art in the service of despotism always rings hollow.

Long since rebuilt, the town is in most respects still as ordinary as the day it was bombed. But now it is awash with artistic symbols – a ceramic mural of Picasso's masterwork, the *Park of the Peoples of Europe*, a sculpture by Henry Moore called *Large Figures in a Shelter* and statues commemorating George Steer, the British journalist whose telegram alerted the world to the bombing and inspired Picasso's response, and Jose Antonio Agirre, the first president of the Basque autonomous community. The attack on Gernika was an attack on people and an attack on an idea, the idea of democracy, that the people of a community can imagine that community for themselves. And the tree – that symbol of people-rule itself – still stands.

Homage to Barcelona

Barcelona, 2005

'I have walked Las Ramblas but not with real intent,' sings James Dean Bradfield of Manic Street Preachers on the only Number One hit single about the International Brigades of the Spanish Civil War and the sense of shame induced by the knowledge that our own useless generation could never repeat such dignity and heroism. Inspired partly by 'If You Tolerate This Your Children Will Be Next', partly by a small monument in Cathays Park honouring those who died, and admittedly partly by the fact that my sister was on her way to Benicassim, a sun-kissed version of Glastonbury Festival further down the Spanish coast, I decided to visit Barcelona and walk Las Ramblas for myself.

Another inspiration for my trip – for it is books, I find, that make you want to do things – was George Orwell's *Homage to Catalonia*. By turns a war story, a travelogue, a historical document, a diary, a memoir and a political tract, Orwell's book stands as a unique record of a unique conflict and a lasting monument to the bravery of those who believed, heroically, that 'if [they] could shoot rabbits [they] could shoot fascists'. The Spanish Civil War lives on in the popular imagination (see also Picasso and The Clash) as the last war of ideas: a conflict which saw young idealists like Orwell give up perfectly comfortable lives in their own countries to travel to Spain and join the fight against Franco.

Homage to Catalonia sheds light on their sacrifice, and also on the tragic infighting between various factions of the Left. Thankfully, Orwell avoids getting too bogged down in the ridiculous ideological differences between the myriad anarchist, communist and socialist groups which led to the self-destruction of any real resistance to Franco's regime, and instead paints a picture of a tragic, heroic, shambolic and profoundly human conflict.

Orwell himself was shot through the neck for the cause, and his oddly philosophical account of this event is one of the most interesting passages in the book: 'There must have been about two minutes during which I assumed I was killed. And that too was interesting – I mean, it is interesting to know what your thoughts would be at such a time.' He also details his battles with lice, secret police, customs officials, fatigue – and rats (his experience in the trenches would give him inspiration for Room 101 in his later, more celebrated, work, *Nineteen Eighty-Four*).

Unsurprisingly, the Ramblas, a series of boulevards that together form the main artery of 'old' Barcelona – running from the central Placa de Catalunya down to the waterfront – is a different set of streets to the ones made famous by George Orwell. Sixty-five years after the Spanish Civil War, and yet less than thirty after the death of Franco released the creative energies of the Catalan people, mercilessly repressed for having chosen the 'wrong' side, the top end of Las Ramblas resembles the busy tourist area of any major city, making me think of Trafalgar Square more than the laid back, bohemian, anarchist city of the guidebooks, coloured by my imagination (quite what the last bastion of romantic anarchism looks like in reality, I don't know).

The same could be said for many of the city's main avenues, crazy blasts of pollution, incomprehensible traffic systems, suicidal scooter-riders and the constant honking of 'anarchist' drivers. But as soon as you step off the most obvious tourist trails, your love affair with the city will begin: whether winding through the narrow, labyrinthine streets of the gothic quarter with its ornate architecture and authentic medieval smell of urine, or riding the modern and efficient metro system out to Gaudi's cathedral. La Sagrada Familia is a huge, crazy, visionary symbol of the city, and is still being built.

Ascending one of its dreaming spires, I found myself in a very slow-moving queue, inching up the stairway step by step as evening sunlight poured through the windows. A lazy Catalan late afternoon melted into a beautiful Catalan early evening. Apart from being a genuine 'been there, done that' world heritage site, there's plenty of graffiti to read on the way up, which, if we put aside its vandalism of the cathedral, offers some interesting ideas from around the world. I even found some Smiths lyrics.

I didn't have time to visit all of Barcelona's many guidebook highlights, but as I'd already decided to go back, I really didn't mind. I did get to the Picasso museum, to which the twentieth-century's greatest artist bestowed most of the work he completed while spending much of his youth in the city, getting inspired by a raucous nightlife centred around the Els Quatre Gats café and a bunch of suitably scruffy bohemian types. The eclectic collection is housed in five medieval mansion houses joined together and includes early drawings and paintings, work from the Blue and Pink periods as well as the world-famous reinterpretations of Velazquez's *Las Meninas*, taking us on a journey from Picasso's earliest work as a fifteen-year-old competition entrant to the invention of Cubism.

One of the most enthusiastic pilgrims on the trail laid down by the writers who documented the Civil War – the trail, I suppose, I was walking myself – has been the Australian art critic Robert Hughes, whose gargantuan tome, *Barcelona*, is almost as comprehensive as its title suggests. Visiting the city 'for the oblique reason [of being] fantastically keen on George Orwell [and wanting] to see the place to which he had paid his homage', Hughes became acquainted with a Catalan sculptor called Xavier Corbero, and soon fell in love with the 'dark narrow bookshops in the Barri Gòtic' and the 'populist paradise' of the fish restaurants in the port.

Beginning with a series of highly personal pen portraits of life in a city obsessed with design, nationalism and transvestites, Hughes soon launches into two thousand years of history as impressive in scope and ambition as Peter Ackroyd's much-vaunted *London: The Biography*. In fact, this type of book – a mammoth attempt at fusing political, economic and social history with analysis of cultural production, by being at once monolithic and anecdotal – already seems like the new way to write about cities. *Barcelona* the book seems to personify Barcelona the city: its broad division into two parts, simply 'The Old City' and 'The New City', is further subdivided into major historical currents which have washed over it, each leaving its own residue: Roman, Visigoth, Frankish, Moorish. In terms of the twentieth-century, Gaudí particularly, along with Picasso, Miró and others are all well-represented, but the beauty of Hughes' book is the labyrinth of uncharted territory into which he leads the reader, uncovering anecdotes and intrigue that lay untouched even by Catalan historians.

Despite being a city which inspired and houses some of the world's greatest art and architecture, one Catalan institution is better-known by foreigners and better-loved by locals than any other: FC Barcelona. If Robert Hughes takes as his starting point the 'truism that all cities are shaped by politics... true to a spectacular and insistent degree of Barcelona,' and applies this statement to art and architecture, Jimmy Burns does the exact same thing with regard to football. Like Hughes, he begins with a personal passion and goes on to provide the reader with a rollercoaster ride through the turbulent history of the 'potent symbol of political and cultural identity' that is FC Barcelona.

Like Hughes, and so many other non-Catalans enchanted by the city and its fierce, often bizarre blend of eccentricity, egalitarianism and exhibitionism, Burns' passion is rooted in the politics of the civil war. An Englishman who grew up in the shadow of Real Madrid's Santiago Bernabeu stadium, he rejected the all-white all-stars because of that club's links to the Franco regime, choosing instead to support the *blaugranas* from the Catalan capital, unable to wave their own flags or speak their own language. *Barca: a people's passion* details the rivalry between two clubs which, for decades, represented the only chance for Catalonia to vent its frustration and express its pride. In the dark years of dictatorship, the club became worthy of its motto – *Som mes que un club* (We're more than a club). Barca was adopted as a vehicle of resistance.

Franco's death in 1975 marked a watershed in both the political and socio-cultural history of the region and the fortunes of the club. Testimony to the club's importance to locals and tourists alike is the fact that I am able to wander into and around the Museu Picasso at leisure, whereas the Camp Nou tour was three times as expensive and had ten times the queue. It was here – at Europe's largest football stadium – that I felt most acutely aware of being inadequately European, ashamed of my British insularity. I listened to some Dutch lads enthusing with a Spaniard, in English, about Cruyff and Neeskens, and wished I were able to talk to the Germans, in French, about Gabbidon and Earnshaw.

And finally, after a metro ride and an ascent up a hill so steep there are escalators in the pavements, Parc Guell. This is where Gaudi turned his hand to landscape gardening, full of palm trees and weird and wonderful mosaic-encrusted monuments. It offers a space to relax and take in panoramic views of the city: a city of balconies and evening sunshine, singing birds and tree-lined boulevards, marketplaces and tapas bars, kids playing basketball and men playing *petanque*, blue skies, and the smells of urine and fish.

A space to think. I had gone to think one thing, and ended up thinking another. It's not what you learn about a city, it's what being in the city can teach you about yourself. Orwell found out the hard way, joining a war in which idealism itself imploded, but we would almost certainly not have *Nineteen Eighty-Four*, one of the twentieth-century's most potent warnings against totalitarianism, without his experiences here. Robert Hughes and Jimmy Burns also ended up staying in Barcelona for reasons different to the ones for which they arrived. And I too was taught a small and humbling lesson: trying to hear the echoes of the days of '39, I heard nothing but my own footsteps taking me back home.

Postcards from Sevilla

Seville, 2011

Winding through streets and alleys and crossing the occasional square, past *bodegas* and *tavernas* and *cervecerias*, eventually we happen upon it. Outside, there is the stamping of feet and the clapping of hands; inside, rows of cinema seats and a dimly-lit bar stacked high with spirits. We'd seen the flyposters taped on walls around the town, simple A4 photocopies with a blurred picture of a dancer. Now we're here, at Bustos Tavera No. 11, we're glad we made the effort: the bar looks like flamenco's answer to an indie club.

It is a poky little place; a low ceiling is held up by pillars on which letters and numbers have been randomly chalked and the low lighting is achieved through clouds of bottles that surround each of the lights. We head straight to the bar and order Cruzcampo, the local beer. Around us, there is a low-key buzz of the kind I recognise from events I have organised myself; you get the impression most of the people here know each other, or know somebody connected to the show. A few other tourists have evidently wandered in having seen the posters – some older couples, a family of three – but the core audience here is from the university, a mix of local and foreign students.

Eventually, the guitarist, or *toque*, appears. He has dark, weather-beaten skin, wizened, gaunt features, hair scraped backwards from a high forehead. He strums out some rhythms. Next, the voice of the *cantaore* rises from a hum to a howl; the singer is a man of about fifty, only just beginning to grey, a smart black shirt covering an ample midriff. Between each passionate outburst, you can hear the disparate influences of this singular style. Beyond the closed and concentrating eyes and the folded hand gestures, you can feel how much it means to these people to keep the rhythm alive.

As the interplay between *toque* and *cantaore* grows more intense, the quick-clapping attains mesmeric power. From the crowd there are shouts of '*oyez!*' From the shadows enter two *bailaoras*, the dancers. Compared to the traditional polka-dot flamboyance we'd seen in the souvenir shops, there is something that seems authentic about the drab colours the two young women have chosen.

The first dancer, smiling and curvaceous, is dressed in black. Flamboyant and graceful, she twists and turns with style and ease. The audience are transfixed; I fall a little bit in love. The other girl is younger; we recognise her from the door. It seems that she has organised this evening; it was she who was friendly and helpful when we began the evening sitting at the wrong end of the room, telling us in a stream of words we didn't understand where to sit to gain the best view. She was friendly, warm and helpful. Her stage persona is different. Her simple, ageless dress is black and brown and, along with the serious look on her face, gives her the severe, hard-faced quality of a nineteenth-century servant-girl.

Where the first dancer – my beauty – had enjoyed the attentions of the crowd in a joyous, celebratory way, there is something confrontational about this second girl. Her twists and turns and even the tiniest of her hand gestures are incendiary. She has a magnetism we associate with rock stars. Having witnessed just two flamenco dancers in my life, I can already tell that each woman has her own distinctive style. The first was Kylie; the second is Mick Jagger. As she freestyles an outro and the crowd call raucously for an encore, I feel sure I've caught a glimpse of *duende* – the soul of the dance.

Afterwards, the guitarist sidles up to the bar. The imported audience files out quickly. I sip my Cruzcampo, hoping the *bailaoras* might be persuaded to have a drink. My head is full of beer and broken Spanish. I catch another sight of Mick, but she is chatting to friends; Kylie, and the moment, has gone.

Taking an evening stroll through the historic quarters of Sevilla, a pedestrianised zone of tramlines, bicycles and bustling tapas bars, we turn a corner of the Iglesia de la Magdalena and happen upon a very strange event. We are not sure whether it is a rehearsal or the real thing.

Our path is blocked by a clutch of photographers crouching in the doorway of this imposing edifice. The gigantic wooden doors are only marginally ajar. From inside the church, there is the whiff of incense and a glimpse of gold. A huge table shuffles forward, a platform carried as if it were the Ark of the Covenant by men in white robes, their faces invisible beneath the intricate carvings on the heavy wood façade. Despite the number of men involved – a couple of dozen at least, crammed like tinned fish beneath the platform – they hardly move. As the photographers retreat, the advance is step by painstaking step, accompanied by much jostling and the unhelpful advice of bystanders.

Back in Wales, I could only assume this was a particularly audacious robbery (round my way, when the price of lead went up, the local church roofs came down); here in Andalusia, I've already learned to accept that this could be anything. Saints' days come thick and fast; they love a good ritual here.

We check the poster on the outside of the church. As far as we can tell, what we are witnessing is something called the Jubilear Circular, or at least a rehearsal for it; our suspicion is all but confirmed when the table, stacked high with irregular shaped objects covered in a white sheet, suddenly disappears around the corner. It would appear that this particular tradition involves taking the furniture on a lap of the church.

All day I've been remarking on the strange figures stacked high in the souvenir shops, crammed between the flamenco dancers, the bulls and the matadors; they are hooded, dressed all in white, with holes only for the eyes. Their hoods are pointed and they carry torches or giant matches. To me, they look like Klansmen; I don't really want one as a fridge magnet.

We have just missed Semana Santa, Seville's celebration of Holy Week, and the discovery that the showpiece event of this famous fiesta is the march of the *nazarenos* – in many ways the original Klansmen – through the city's streets makes me relieved not to have witnessed this sinister spectacle.

I jump to conclusions. I assume that these were the vigilantes of the Inquisition; I know that in this part of Spain they still celebrate the *reconquista*, the Catholic-Christian victory over the Iberian Moors. Given the world's current tensions between Christendom and Islam, and the proximity of North Africa, such anachronism seems full only of vengeance and spite. But then, I am ill-informed; I am judging an event I haven't seen on the sole basis that it features men in pointy hoods. I remind myself that my inexplicable discomfort with Catholic iconography would be reciprocated perhaps by a Spaniard witnessing Britain's annual celebration of Protestant supremacism, where we eat hotdogs while an effigy of a Catholic insurrectionist burns.

The fact that nobody in modern Britain sees the fifth of November in such terms, despite that everybody knows the date should speak volumes. Guido Fawkes serves as a reminder not only of gunpowder, treason and plot, but perhaps more importantly as a warning not to judge the traditions of others by their origins. Sometimes you really can divorce an event from its context.

The same could not, however, be said of bullfighting, which is not a celebration of past tortures, rather an enactment in the present. *Torture ni arte* claims the lone 'anti' sticker in the vicinity of the Plaza de Toros de la Maestranza de Caballería de Sevilla, Spain's oldest bullring, across the road from the river Guadalquivir. For the vast majority of Sevillanos, it is not an ancient rite like the procession of the *nazarenos*, simply a part of everyday life.

Like foxhunting in many rural areas of Great Britain, it is part spectacle, part theatre, but it is ingrained in the culture; whatever the progressive perception, these 'sports' do not need or appreciate the inverted commas. Not, at least, to the people involved. A mixed crowd streams steadily toward the ring; there is the heightened air that accompanies the build-up to a football match. But nobody is shouting or waving flags; there is no showy emotion. If we are determined to make an analogy, it is like the crowd outside a West End show.

I don't enter the arena. I'm sure I'd enjoy the atmosphere but quickly lose the thrill once the maiming gets underway. I'm no Hemingway.

I've come to Andalusia to escape the Royal Wedding, but all societies are bound up in ritual. All culture, to varying degrees, is pomp and ceremony, to which we ascribe our own meanings. Some people might feel at home lining London avenues to wave Union Jacks, others watching bulls being spiked in the bullrings of Seville. Me? I'm happiest sitting here at a café table, taking it all in. Sunlight, beer and conversation, living and letting live.

The Sun Also Rises

Pamplona, 2015

'San Fermin,' says Mikel, 'is like Sodom and Gomorrah: sex in the streets, alcohol, drugs.' It is a description of the event that makes a sharp contrast with the images of the fiesta that line the streets of Pamplona, the city's most famous event celebrated with T-shirts depicting cartoon bulls, photographs of laughing bull-runners (none of whom are getting gored) and a full gamut of the usual tourist tat. But there is little reason to doubt Mikel's word; his modest bookshop-café opens out onto the Plaza Consistorial, a little square that is just a short stampede to Pamplona's main open space, where last month's festivities began, and where, nearly eighty years ago, Hemingway sat in the Café Iruña and turned the events of that summer into *The Sun Also Rises*, one of my favourite books.

We had entered Mikel's café the previous evening, on our *paseo* mission to find an English-language bookshop, but finding the only text in stock not in Castilian or Basque to be the very edition of *Fiesta: The Sun Also Rises* that I have on my shelves at home, we swiftly moved on. But now, wanting a comfort stop and a coffee, we are once again seduced by the look of the place: white minimalist shelving, a small collection of books and magazines arranged to make it look as if it is quite okay to take them down and read over a *café con leche*, and an intriguing wall-length map of the Atlantic Ocean, with the eastern Americas visible in the west and Europe and the western portion of Africa in the east.

I order a coffee for myself and ask about the tea options for my wife, who is missing home comforts and having to make do with *infusiones* in mint and berry flavours when all she wants is a basic cuppa. Mikel susses our Britishness – despite my basic Spanish, it cannot be a difficult task – and immediately recommends a Pakistani black tea, which Chantelle is more than happy to try. He even offers a little milk on the side, and switches to near-perfect English, so by the time the tea arrives, brewing nicely in an ornate cast-iron pot with a looping handle, I feel we are bosom buddies, especially given the particularly slow, particularly curt service we have been receiving on some of the tourist *terrazas*.

Mikel has already shown himself to be a man of knowledge when we told him where we are from: he is a big fan of Ryan Giggs and we spend a moment reminiscing about Mark Hughes' time at Barcelona in the 1980s. The two Welsh players he singles out may suggest some Manchester United affiliation, but I'm willing to forgive my new friend even that, given that he has performed the miracle of sourcing my wife a lovely cup of tea.

And besides, being a man after my own heart, Mikel is soon regaling us, between attending to other customers sitting at the two or three tables he has outside in the square, about the things he really cares about. We learn that he is from Venezuela, a place called Cumanà, which is the oldest European city in the whole of Latin America; he points it out on the map, a short hop from Trinidad.

The café, Al Norte del Sur – 'At the North of the South', has only been open for two weeks – from the finale of San Fermin, the bull-running festival. Its rather odd name refers to the geography of Mikel's story, which he admits is 'a novel'. His grandparents were originally from Bilbao – in the north of the south of Europe – but were forced to flee Franco's advance during the Spanish Civil War. 'Twenty-five thousand refugees from Spain settled in Venezuela during the civil war,' Mikel informs us, an aspect of the conflict that had previously escaped my attention. 'And many, many more in Argentina.'

The reason Mikel's story is novel material, and the reason it is his story as well as that of his antecedents is that he has now returned to the land of his fathers, with his wife and three children, to escape the crisis in Venezuela. My new friend does not elaborate beyond the fact that 'it is really sad; it is not a place to bring up children', but the fact that he has swapped his old life as a Professor of Biology for one waiting tables in a square full of tourists, hustlers and buskers suggests it is one he was forced to make.

Mikel is full of surprises, one minute giving a potted family saga spread across centuries and continents, the next chatting affably with locals who have clearly taken to their new gregarious and warm-hearted neighbour. 'I have no problem doing this,' Mikel says of waiting tables. 'Since I was a little boy, every weekend my parents would have big reunions and I would always be the one to go around – you know, with a tray.' It is a touching picture, another glimpse of a scene from the novel of Mikel's life.

In the time it takes me to drink a cup of strong coffee and for my wife to indulge herself with a second cup of tea, we have touched on football, politics, religion, history, geography – and the enormous benefits of drinking non-alcoholic beer. Unlicensed, Al Norte del Sur has four different varieties on offer. I plump for an Amstel and listen intently as Mikel tells me about the natural vitamins and minerals in beer whose positive effects are normally dampened by alcohol.

But it is to the person of San Fermin that we return. Mikel, a man of faith, has clearly been saddened by his arrival in this city in which San Fermin is everywhere and nowhere. The red scarf is worn as traditional costume, along with a white shirt and trousers, to remember St Fermin's martyrdom. You can buy the costume in many of Pamplona's tourist shops, alongside pretty much anything relating to a bull. But Mikel is the only person who tells me the true story – depending, of course, on what you believe – about San Fermin the evangelist and miracle worker, who settled in Amiens, northern France, to – in Mikel's words – 'work for Jesus'.

And this is his mission. To recover San Fermin, and some of the other early saints, characters and legends – most especially for the flow of *peregrinos* – the pilgrims who pass by at the bottom of the square, on their way to Santiago de Compostela, reputed site of the bones of St James, hardly any of whom – in Mikel's view – are doing it for 'religious' reasons. 'For most, it's just tourism,' he says.

Mikel has sent a book for printing – of all places, to Ireland – and is waiting for the return of copies. *In a Virtuous Earth* will sell to pilgrims and passers-by, along with coffee, non-alcoholic beer and the occasional tea. I spend two euros on a postcard depicting the book's back cover and Mikel agrees to send me the pdf. I like its sentiment.

A small red circle contains the 'software' for our being, the key words I am perhaps most comfortable with – 'Mind', 'Sociology', 'Culture' and 'Human' – being dominated by the big blue circle 'hardware' of Mikel's discipline: 'Cells', 'Organs', 'Biology', 'Body', 'Matter'. But both 'hardware' and 'software' are dwarfed in my new friend's schema by the yellow circle of 'energy', comprising 'Soul', 'Spirit' and 'Faith'.

A half-hour with Mikel has provided perhaps half a lifetime's worth of food for thought. We only went in for coffee. And the more I reflect on Mikel's *Virtuous Earth* postcard and his stories of the real San Fermin, the more I am drawn back to the place where Hemingway got his title. Not 'Fiesta' – that is too simple, brutish, full of the pleasures of the flesh – but 'The Sun Also Rises'.

It is taken from the book of *Ecclesiastes*:

> *One generation passeth away, and another generation cometh; but the earth abideth forever... The sun also ariseth, and the sun goeth down, and hasteth to the place where he arose... The wind goeth toward the south, and turneth about unto the north; it whirleth about continually, and the wind returneth again according to its circuits... All the rivers run into the sea; yet the sea is not full; unto the place from whence the rivers come thither they return again.*

Perhaps it is the wisest human sentiment ever committed to parchment. There is nothing – not dictatorships nor refugees, not virtue nor vice, neither coincidences nor accidental friendships, neither belief nor unbelief, nor coffee nor tea – nothing is new under the sun. Especially in Pamplona.

Food for Thought

Logroño, 2015

Despite its handsome architecture and laid-back ambience, the northern Spanish town of Logroño would be unremarkable were it not for its fantastic foodie culture and global reputation for drink. Perhaps I should mention, for those unaware of Logroño and its charms, that it is the principal city of La Rioja, the relatively small autonomous region situated to the south of the Basque Country that produces what is, in my humble, inexpert opinion – simply based on drinking the stuff – the world's finest wine.

Logroño is encircled by *calados* (wine cellars) dating back to the sixteenth-century, when the locals took the wine-making process seriously enough to pass by-laws restricting cart-traffic on those streets with underground cellars so as not to disturb the wine. There are also the world famous *bodegas*, some of which occupy stone buildings dating back centuries -- like that of the Marquès de Murrieta, while others, like the new Campo Viejo winery, opened in 2001, stand as temples to modern viniculture. The Darien winery, on the road out toward Zaragoza, was designed by the avant-garde architect Jésus Marino Pascual; it looks like a spaceship has landed among the vineyards.

Riojans bring the same spirit of adventure and experimentation to food. A weekend-night crawl through the Old Quarter bars of the Calle Laurel and Calle San Juan reveals the beating heart of the city. Neither street name has the global resonance of the region which gives the wine its famous name, but these two back alleys have a growing, and glowing, reputation among food lovers. La Laurel is crammed with over a hundred *pincho* bars, where one can linger over a very reasonably priced *copa* of rioja or a swift *cerveza* while feasting on an inexhaustible array of sumptuous bar snacks, ranging from old tapas favourites – olives, *patatas bravas*, calamari and *jamones ibericos* – to brilliant inventions like *cojonudos* (a fried quail egg with chopped chorizo on bread).

And here in La Laurel, revelling in the buzz of my first true pincho bar-crawl, the quality of the crianzas and the sheer invention of the food-as-art, I am struck by the contrast in nightlife between the British and the Basques and Spanish. Here, approaching midnight on a Saturday, the streets are thronged with families. Local women lean over balconies and shout to their friends in the *calle* below. Kids dart about on scooters. Tough-looking dudes wander in groups eating ice-creams. People eat, walk, talk. The elderly gather on benches to watch their former selves flirting and frolicking. Most of the adults are drinking, but hardly anyone is inebriated.

You will hardly need me to provide a description of the equivalent scene in Britain. A city centre on a Saturday night is sentence enough to conjure the images. The food here is for thought.

My own capital city has an equally celebrated rat-run of late night eateries, but Cardiff's 'Chip Alley' on Caroline Street provides a startling contrast with the sophisticated gastronomes of Logroño. Here the copious consumption of greasy, starchy filler comes as part of the ritual stumble to the taxi rank or the last bus or train. It is not that I don't appreciate chicken off-the-bone, curry, rice and chips, nor indeed fried chicken or doner kebabs. In fact, if push came to shove, I'd take a scotch egg over any fancy soft cheese and caramelised onion delicacy the *pinchoistas* could blow torch for me.

The problem we have in Wales, and the UK more generally, with late-night eating and drinking is not the food itself, or even the alcohol. It is the culture that has grown up around it. In Logroño you can clearly see that everybody likes a drink; equally clearly, you can observe that enjoyment of alcohol goes hand in hand with good food and social rather than antisocial behaviour. Vomiting, fighting and the heavy presence of emergency services are off the menu in Spain. Perhaps we ought to take a cobblestone out of Logroño's back alleys?

Rather than denying the vital contribution the sale of alcohol and junk food make to the so-called 'night-time economy' or denying the ingrained culture of drunkenness that has pervaded British life for centuries, perhaps we could simply trial a different kind of nightlife in a couple of dedicated streets to inspire incremental change?

We have, after all, already begun to adopt a more continental approach to eating and drinking. Despite the frequent inclemency of the weather, around the corner, in Caroline Street's upmarket sister, Mill Lane, Cardiff has created a so-called café quarter. On sunny and not-so-sunny days, people sit outside and enjoy the service of waiters who come to take orders – in sharp contrast to the standing room only super-bars on the opposite side of St Mary Street, where an hour can pass simply waiting to be served. Then you have to negotiate a dancefloor where your pint is more likely than not to be spilled en route to a tiny shelf where it will rest while you fail to hear anything your friends might be attempting to say.

The conversion of the former Brains building into a 'Brewery Quarter' of chain restaurants and bars has already eroded the original character of Caroline Street, and although to some who would like to preserve the authentic Old Cardiff in aspic it may seem like sacrilege to suggest it, maybe it is time we thought about transforming Caroline Street into Wales' premier *pincho* destination. It could be the catalyst for a revolution in late night drinking culture in the whole of the UK, which has – like so much else in British culture – been co-opted by commercial interests at the expense of community.

Imagine popping out with your colleagues for an after-work quarter-pint of beer and a pineapple fritter, or chatting up the girl from the office over a not-so-swift half and a miniature Clark's pie on a bed of mash. There's already 'beer tapas' available on Westgate Street; all we need now is the recognition that a third of a pint is both a more normal volume around most of the world, and is – obviously – far better for our health. Couple it with some – okay, not so healthy – local delicacies and you have a recipe which suits small businesses and the local economy, but also the ordinary punter who might want to stay out late for a pie and a pint and a catch up with friends without necessarily having to fall over.

Fado, Fish and Fernando de Pessoa

Lisbon, 2016

There is a wisdom that says Portugal invented the global village. While that might not be quite true, the country's geographical position, at the very edge of the Old World, did cement its centrality to the great Age of Discovery. From the late fifteenth-century, Portuguese explorers led the way in turning our flat distorted maps into globes we could spin.

The islands of Madeira and the Azores were discovered in the 1420s, following which Henry the Navigator encouraged European ships further and further into the mid Atlantic. Once the psychological barrier of Cape Bojador – in present-day Western Sahara – was passed, and sailors realised their boats would not fan into flame beyond some flat earth apocalypse horizon, West African ports opened up. Forts, trading posts and the slave trade followed.

Global trade routes – trails blazed along the Silk Road, beginning during China's Han dynasty a couple of centuries before Christ – finally took to the high seas. Vasco da Gama rounded Africa, reaching Calicut on the Malabar coast of India, opening up the Indian Ocean and Portuguese outposts across South East Asia. The world would never be the same again, although it was a full century before Europe's imperial powers surpassed Portuguese mastery over the Cape Route.

Arriving in Lisbon on the weekend of the Web Summit, one is immediately struck by how every nation must live in the present. While the tourist trail centres on the castles, palaces and monuments of Portugal's past, Lisbon's residents quietly go about their business as modern European citizens. Kosovan-Albanian-British singer Rita Ora adorns every available advertising space, kitted up in Tezenis underwear, staring sultrily at the camera, Photoshopped into the generic twenty-first-century beauty ideal. At the former Mercado de Ribeira, the international publishing phenomenon that is *Time Out* magazine have given the traditional market a makeover, transforming the place into a pan-global foodie heaven. Digital artisans abound, lanyards swinging freely about their dress-down casual-wear: box-fresh trainers, branded hoodies and impossibly skinny jeans. Just as the ceramicists of yesteryear would have taken a break from painstaking tile arrangements to enjoy fresh fish with crisp white wine, attendees at Web Summit kick back from coding with artisanally arranged sushi-boxes and cool Czech pilsners.

Azulejos, Lisbon's ubiquitous tiles, are remnants of a Moorish past. Long, wide pavements are entirely constructed from these often intricately patterned tiles. They evoke a sense of *saudade*, Portuguese *hiraeth*, a 'missingness' befitting a small country whose sailors were sometimes away for years, often dying in shipwrecks or finding new loves and new homes in far flung corners of the global village they helped to build. Lisbon retains a faint air of resignation, a subdued atmosphere you would do well to find in any city of equivalent size in the country's larger, brasher Iberian neighbour. If Spain is light and noise, Portugal is quality of light and echoes.

At night, the hilly, cobbled streets of the Alfama district, a ramshackle yellow tram ride away above the seafront, come alive with the melancholic strains of *fado*. 'On one side we have the Spanish with their swords; on the other side there's the sea,' explained its most famous exponent, Amalia Rodrigues. 'When people set sail we were waiting and suffering, so *fado* is a complaint.'

Coffee, note-taking and people watching are best done at Berard's, where the *pasteles de nata*, the famous Portuguese custard tarts, are served perfectly alongside a *pingado* (somewhere in the just-a-dash hinterland between an Italian *macchiato* and a Spanish *cortado*). A little way down the Rua Garrett is Bertrand's, which doesn't simply purport to be the oldest bookshop in the world – it proudly displays a Guinness World Record certificate to accompany its proud boast of having been founded in 1732.

I pick up a book. 'In a time which celebrates fame, success, stupidity, convenience and noise,' writes John Lanchester in the *Daily Telegraph*, 'here is the perfect antidote.' It is the first of four excerpts from the British press that adorn the Serpent's Tail Classics edition of *The Book of Disquiet* by Fernando de Pessoa. The book has appealed to me not only because of the prominence Pessoa's works are given here at Bertrand, but because today is a day of disquiet.

Donald Trump has been elected as the 45th President of the United States of America, and the rest of the world is, while carrying on with business as usual, holding its breath and waiting to see what happens next. Lanchester's five giants – fame, success, convenience, stupidity and noise – find themselves incarnate in the man who self-styles as The Donald, and who – however sober and conciliatory a tone he strikes today – has built an election campaign and career on these anti-virtues.

After the Second World War, the Attlee government rebuilt Britain by aiming to vanquish the scourges of want, disease, ignorance, squalor and idleness. It would seem that Trump's plan to 'Make America Great Again' is built on nothing more substantial than repeating this mantra, offending a lot of people and ensuring a lot of noise.

We watch the mini-apocalypse on a news-channel loop, dubbed into Portuguese on a small-screen television in a three-star Lisbon hotel room, its décor bang up to date if only we were watching Reagan's second term swearing-in. Then we go out in search of grilled fish. The faint strains of *fado* from a bar are drowned out by hip-hop from a passing car, reminding us that, however disquieting the vagaries of history, the world will continue to spin.

The Protestant Cemetery

Rome, 2008

I used to have a habit – some might call it an obsession – with checking the biographical details of writers I was reading. What concerned me was not where they were born or where they lived or whether they were married, but when they had had their first book published or when they'd written their first poem. As you get older, of course, you find more and more writers were younger than you when they made their big breakthrough, and so I forced myself to stop checking, as it would only make me depressed.

The really depressing thing about John Keats – if viewed from this, admittedly, skewed perspective – is not so much the age he was when Leigh Hunt published his first sonnets in *The Examiner* (he was twenty, if you must know) but the enormity of his poetic achievement considering he didn't even make it to twenty-seven, that mythical age when the great and the good (Rupert Brooke, Robert Johnson, Jimi Hendrix et al) are supposedly at their most susceptible. Many poets would give their right eye to have written just one of Keats' great odes by the age of twenty-five (he wrote them all that year) or 'The Eve of St Agnes' at any point in their career. But by twenty-six, Keats had published fifty-four poems – many of them masterpieces – and taken off for the next world, leaving us only to wonder quite how large he might have loomed in English letters were he to have been allowed to us for his full three score and ten.

So it is with a heavy heart, and just a smidgeon of jealousy, that

I make the pilgrimage to Rome, not to visit the palaces of once-great emperors or to seek an audience with the Pope, not to queue with the hordes at the Sistine Chapel or to wave scarves and flags in the Stadio Olimpico, but to seek out a walled cemetery in an obscure part of the city. This is where the city's non-Catholics are buried, and here lie the bones of two of England's finest poets.

I come to Rome's Protestant Cemetery hoping to see the graves of Keats and Shelley, but the work ethic, it seems, doesn't extend to the keeper of the graveyard. The sign to which a distinguished Italian gentleman in a long black trench coat refers indicates that the cemetery is supposed to close at 12.30 on Mondays. It is already ten to one, and he is only now locking the gate. 'Can we go in?' I ask, in English, indicating that the gate he holds in his hand is, even now, not yet utterly locked. He shakes his head with a thin smile, firm but fair. '*Lunedi chiuso,*' he repeats, 'Mondays is a close.'

He disappears around a corner and I am left standing disappointed in the sweltering heat, observing nothing but a major road junction, considering how long it has been since I passed a pizzeria. There is nothing for it but to turn back.

I know what Keats' monument looks like anyhow. Its inscription is possibly *the* most famous on a writer's grave, a tragic yet ambiguous line, which opens up several controversies:

Here lies One Whose Name was Writ in Water

This was the line penned by the poet himself as he lay dying in the house on the Spanish Steps. Sunlight, of course, was no cure for tuberculosis. Keats, once apprenticed to a surgeon himself, knew he was doomed: he recognised the dark shade of the arterial blood he was coughing. Famously, it was the poet's friends, Joseph Severn and Charles Brown, who added – to their later regret – a contextualisation for Keats' wish:

This Grave contains all that was mortal of a YOUNG ENGLISH POET who on his Death Bed, in the Bitterness of his heart, at the Malicious Power of his enemies, desired these words to be Engraven on his Tomb Stone

They had taken his instruction as a tragic admission that in the wake of a series of searing criticisms of 'Endymion', their friend had resigned himself to oblivion. Shelley even went so far as to blame the *Quarterly Review* critic who had laid into Keats for the death of his companion and fellow-poet, prompting Byron – who never met Keats – to write, probably in sardonic riposte to Shelley's recasting of Keats as 'Adonais': 'snuffed out by an article'.

Oscar Wilde can't have visited on a Monday, for he, famously, had chance to fall at Keats' grave and weep, later penning a poem on 'The Grave of Keats' which ended 'Thy name was writ in water – it shall stand / And tears like mine will keep thy memory green'. Well, thanks Oscar, I like to think Keats might have said, but we'll leave my work to do that. And so, on Melancholy:

Aye, in the vey temple of Delight
  Veiled Melancholy has her sovereign shrine,
    Though seen of none save him whose strenuous tongue
  Can burst Joy's grape against his palate fine,
His soul shall taste the sadness of her might,
  And be among her cloudy trophies hung.

Postcard from the Renaissance

Florence, 2008

Just take a look at the legacy bequeathed to us. Four hundred years after they were painstakingly painted onto the ceilings and walls of chapels and churches and cathedrals, human beings are still gazing in wonder, despite that almost all of their spiritual power has evaporated, lost to a more secularised appreciation of the fine arts.

Here at Il Duomo in Florence, the centre of the Renaissance, that rebirth and rekindling of the relationship between man and God, religion and painting captured in Leonardo da Vinci's connecting fingers, the decline of belief (and respect) is borne out by the graffiti covering the walls.

The ceiling of the gigantic dome depicts *The Last Judgement*, with celestial beings, angels of white and gold combining beauty and power at the apex of the dome whilst below a host of gruesome devils and horned beasts take pleasure in maiming and roasting the damned. It is the latter part of the panorama to which my eye is drawn, mainly I think because this is the part I recognise: my own time is full of such images, from Rwanda and Guantanamo to *Call of Duty* and the *Texas Chainsaw Massacre*. To an extent, we are desensitised to the violence and the horror of torture because the world we live in is itself a kind of hell. If we are not victims or perpetrators, we are the guilty who sit idly by, getting our fix from television and the internet.

Of the paintings on the ceiling of the Dome, it is the heavenly ones we no longer recognise. White Europe is the most godless place on Earth. We like art and culture but we no longer do religion. The Renaissance was followed by the Enlightenment and the *Origin of Species*.

So how will our era be defined? What will be our legacy? What will survive the early twenty-first century to be wondered at by future generations?

To consider these questions – or worse, the answers – is to stare straight into the abyss. It is to realise that the minds of our forebears were, quite literally, on higher things. Almost all of the art and architecture of Renaissance Italy is designed to make us look up, to contemplate the heavens and admit our finite mortality in an infinite universe. There are domes and towers and spires and pillars and columns and statues with eyes raised heavenwards, hands lifted in exaltation.

And now? Our religion is capitalism, I'm afraid. Our gods are shallow celebrities and worthless material goods. Our finest art is advertising. Our equivalent of Michaelangelo's *David* is David Beckham stripped to his briefs, airbrushed in moody black-and-white to advertise underwear.

There was nothing more sobering than having descended the spiral staircase at Il Duomo to find a window obscured by a sticker applied by someone from back home. It was round, yellow and emblazoned with the letters *glc* and a phrase that may have baffled most visitors but that I recognised only too well.

'You knows it', it said. And I suppose I do.

Piazza San Marco

Venice, 2008

Why is it I find myself willing to buy a one-euro bag of pigeon-feed for my son to throw willy-nilly for the greedy birds which flock the piazza, and yet unable to part with the same small sum for the brown-faced gypsy girl who roams the square begging, in the original, desperate, pleading, imploring sense of the word?

All of life is here in the piazza on a sunlit afternoon in late spring. In front of the famous Florian café, waiters in white tuxedos glide between the tables holding silver trays loaded with overpriced drinks; tourists flock like the pigeons: kissing, taking photographs, posing, buying souvenirs, sipping overpriced beer or coffee; there are the street-vendors, the hawkers, the hagglers, the pickpockets and the beggars: all part of the picture, all in their own ways trying to wheedle what they can from whatever change people have left.

The eyes of the girl are a deep shade of brown. They are sad eyes, too old for her young face. She looks at me imploringly. 'Please,' she begs in English, holding out an empty polystyrene cup. 'I am hungry,' she continues, her voice becoming more desperate. She steps closer, holds the cup right in front of me. '*Please*,' she repeats.

I am moved, but I do not move. Is it the theatricality of this familiar tableau that prevents my hand reaching my pocket? There is none of the shame inherent in the muttered requests of the bearded men who sit in the shop doorways and subways of my own city: their quiet desperation has somehow become part of the backdrop to British life; the high street wouldn't quite be the same without a few *Big Issue* sellers, their red tabards lend them a strange legitimacy which simultaneously softens and hardens our attitude to their plight. In their poverty, the homeless Brit loses none of his or her quintessential reserve; if anything, the shame and hopelessness make it more acute: theirs are hunches and stoops, a body language of the beaten. But here, in the shadow of a cathedral, in a strange and atmospheric city of shadows and bridges and dark canals, the destitute look you in the eye.

There are all too many plausible excuses for not giving to a beggar: maybe she's cheating, lying to you, perhaps she's a fraud; maybe you don't have any change (what's stopping you giving a note?)... well, in any case, where do you stop? If you gave a euro to every beggar, you'd soon be a beggar yourself. Her gestures – the way she holds the pathetic cup, the melodramatic look on her face, the throwing out of arms – each is as hollow as my own holding out of supposedly empty pockets. Perhaps.

I say perhaps because somewhere amid all the things that separate us – the language barrier, the crowd of pigeons about our feet, the differences in class and race and gender and nationality – somewhere there is a connection. As we look into each others' eyes, the gypsy girl and I, we see each others' whole lives. I want to invoke cliché, to say simply that we are worlds apart, but here the phrase is meaningless. Here in the Piazza San Marco, we collide.

'Please,' she says again, '*please*'. And in the moment I turn away, something about humanity is encapsulated: my protestations and empty claims of empty pockets are not inhuman. Sadly, my reaction is *all too* human. The wave of genuine pity and compassion that washes over me comes only afterwards, and inevitably, it is mixed with guilt.

As my son scatters bird-feed across the square and the brass band outside the Florian strike up another tune, I scan the crowd, in a panic, wanting to unburden myself of this wretched coin, but the girl has vanished. I will never see her again, and anyway, a euro is worth even less as a second thought. I feel as small as the coin I wouldn't give away and which, even now, burns a hole in my hand.

Libreria Acqua Alta

Venice, 2008

Venice is renowned for its beauty and its charming character, the latter perhaps being a euphemism for its audacity, its utterly unlikely craziness. So it is perhaps unsurprising that the Libreria Acqua Alta, said by some to be the world's most beautiful bookshop, shares this distinctive quality too. Like almost everything else in Venice, it is at its best when simply happened upon. This is how I discovered it. Soaking up the gorgeous feeling of being lost among bridges and alleyways and canals, the bookshop just kind of appeared.

It has everything a bibliophile could ask for: a ramshackle cavern of books and maps and prints haphazardly strewn on shelves and trestle tables, and a cat whose purpose seems to be reclining in the sunlight amid piles of postcards and adding to the lazy feel of this backstreet.

And the centrepiece? A gondola brimming with books. Of course! It's surprising how many books a gondola can hold. Almost as amazing as how much time one is able to while away browsing in such a place as this. I dip my hand into the gondola and bring out some of the literary history of this fascinating city, a place unique in the world and in world literature.

Henry James called Venice 'the repository of consolations'; Gore Vidal thought it perfect for 'someone looking for a heart to break'. It's a city for lovers – candlelit restaurants along the Grand Canal or holding hands in the Piazza San Marco – but love *affairs*, not marriage. A simple stroll around the city is enough to break your heart: imperial grandeur not so much faded as cracked and withered, an air of resignation, melancholia, decay.

Love in Venice is lost love, unrequited love, doomed love; it is never happily ever after. In Hemingway's *Across the River and Into the Trees*, the bitter retired colonel has a brief affair with a nineteen-year-old contessa knowing that he is going to die soon. Similarly, Gustav von Aschenbach's obsession with the boy Tadzio in Thomas Mann's *Death in Venice* is one of fleeting glances and degradation, given the perfect backdrop by the city's labyrinth. Likewise Daphne Du Maurier's short story which Nicholas Roeg turned into the film *Don't Look Now*: Venice is a place of mystery, hidden threats, glimpses and deceit. Affairs and death hang over Henry James' *The Wings of a Dove*; like the couple in Ian McEwan's *The Comfort of Strangers*, fictional visitors to Venice seem unable to avoid being drawn into dark water and dead ends.

The gondola of Venetian fiction may be overflowing with death and psychological unravelling, but the store itself is anything but. The owner sits among his cats, hardly having time to glance at the folded newspaper on his desk between multilingual conversations with the tourists from Britain, France, Spain, Germany and the rest of Italy as they browse, wide-eyed, clutching their colourful, sinister souvenir carnival masks.

At the rear of the store is a sight more strange and spectacular than the gondola. *Acqua Alta* means 'high water', something Venetians know more than a little about. The back doors of the store, propped open with a pair of oars, open straight out onto the murky green water of a canal. Again, this should not come as a surprise: this is Venice, after all, where the streets are made of water.

But it is not the *fact* of the canal that shocks, rather its proximity to this treasure trove of printed matter: antiquarian maps, first edition art criticism and secondhand textbooks. Green water laps at the back steps. Even a miniscule rise in the water level could precipitate catastrophe. A single thunderstorm – not a rare occurrence on the lagoon – would necessitate sandbags and the hasty restocking of shelves.

But this is precisely what gives Libreria – and Venice – its charm: beauty – and eccentricity – under constant threat of destruction. We sometimes forget, in our cosseted lives, that this is the position of human civilisation; we are only ever one step from catastrophe. A canal laps at our back door too.

On the Platform at Monfalcone

Monfalcone, 2008

The train from Trieste to Ljubljana is not exactly straightforward; in fact, it's not really a train from Trieste to Ljubljana. It's a long wait in a little station in a place called Monfalcone.

If, as Jan Morris suggests in her book *Trieste and the Meaning of Nowhere*, Trieste is a melancholy city because its heyday as principal port of the Austro-Hungarian Empire is over and because it occupies a position on a slither of no-man's land where Latin, Slav and Teutonic cultures fizzle out into the Adriatic – if indeed Trieste is nowhere – then Monfalcone, which seems to be comprised entirely of the railway station and multitudinous sulphurous industrial works, lies outside of nowhere.

It is in Monfalcone that I meet Samir. And it is stops like this in places like this that always seem to provide the backdrop for stories like these. A chance encounter on a railway platform. Our paths crossing for the first – and surely the only – time. We strike up conversation to – in Samir's phrase – 'fill time'. Filling time is very important for Samir.

I know a little about Slovenia, enough to engender the conversation with some context; he knows less about Wales – 'Is it in Australia? No, no, the one near London' – but that is hardly the point.

Samir has been in a 'community' in a small town in Tuscany since the December before last, and in all that time has not been back home to Ljubljana. He has not seen his mother, his brother or his fiancée. In fact, his fiancée didn't even realise he was going until he had gone. Despite Samir's rare and arresting openness, it takes me a little while to understand that the 'community' he talks of is rehab.

Samir is clean now and speaks with huge emotion between drags on a Camel Light about how much he is looking forward to seeing his mother. He has been clean before, but last time felt like he was serving time in the community after his mother had sent him there at the age of eighteen without a choice. That was after he had sold his shoes in order to score and his family finally had to entrust him to outside help. It's amazing how much you can learn about someone's life in one half-hour conversation, especially if they are as open and honest as Samir.

He is twenty-five 'this time', he tells me, and ready to start again. I believe him too. He looks older than his years, which is hardly surprising, but focused too. I feel privileged to have been able to talk to somebody so clearly aware of the fact that his life is at a crossroads.

Here on the platform at Monfalcone, I've been inconvenienced by an hour's hiatus in my holiday, but Samir is awaiting the beginning of the rest of his life. After eighteen months in 'the community', a train from Florence to Venice and a missed train at half past six this morning, it must seem like nothing to wait for an hour for a two-and-a-half hour train which will take him home to his mother, and then – on Friday – to Bosnia, to stay with his brother and his wife and daughter, where he will finally be reunited with his fiancée, who, he says, has waited for him all this time.

No, the wait in Monfalcone is not long, though I can see from the way Samir talks – in measured tones between long drags on his cigarette – and from the pain in his eyes and from the small teardrop tattooed on the piece of skin between his thumb and forefinger that this has been the longest, darkest journey. I cannot wait to see him step off the train in Ljubljana, back into the sunlight of his homeland.

It is not just our personal lives we discuss in the heat and smoke of the plastic shelter on Platform 2 at Monfalcone. Samir wonders how I got hold of my English newspaper: yesterday's *Guardian* in which I was in the middle of reading a review of the new *Encyclopaedia of Wales*.

We talk about the meaning of our names: mine taken from a poet of whom he hasn't heard via a folk singer of whom he has. The fact that his name is not ethnic Slovene leads us inevitably toward the other dark shadow that has been hanging over our conversation, as if heroin addiction was not enough. Samir's name is Turkish and he reveals, with marginally less frankness than before, that he is a Muslim, though neither he nor his family practice. He is careful to qualify this secular status: 'If I was in Bosnia, I would feel guilty,' he says, 'there I would go to the mosque with everybody else.'

My mental arithmetic says he was seven when Slovenia gained independence, the first former Yugoslav republic to do so, following a ten-day struggle in 1991, a precursor to the longer, more horrific tragedies that were to befall her neighbours in Bosnia and Croatia. I ask if he remembers much about the war. Samir's reply is brief and heartfelt; in saying next to nothing, he actually says it all: 'I know what they did to us.'

He tells me how his father used to hit him over the head with a rolled up newspaper every time Bosnia came on TV, presumably to try to protect his son from the reports of atrocities across the border. Again, he avoids talking directly: the pain of being hit with a newspaper displaces the unmentionable. Unlike with his own personal problems, he is quick to change the subject.

'Things are much better now,' he says, 'especially since the Euro.' It is a refreshing thing to hear, out here at this small station at the crossroads of Europe, in the absence of *The Sun* and the *Daily Mail*: somebody from a small, relatively new country of 'two, two-and-a-half million people,' taking pride in the fact that their country is currently president of the EU.

In so many ways Samir represents the new Europe: a Muslim and an ethnic Turk who is proud of his Slovenia, a country that did not even exist when he was born; a man who speaks four languages pretty perfectly; a man who has made some very bad mistakes in his life, but is all the more determined to put them right. Certainly, Samir was the perfect person to meet in Monfalcone.

Thinking of him now, I remember yet another story he told me when he was opening up, completely unprompted, about his drug addiction: he talked of a fifty-year old guy whom he'd met on that very platform the first time he returned from 'the community'. This guy had beaten a habit of twenty-one years, and offered Samir at least a glimpse of what it might be like to escape the vicious circle he'd been witnessing in 'the community'.

'He's my inspiration,' Samir told me.

I didn't get to see him greet his mother on the platform at Ljubljana, but something tells me that if Samir the person is anything like as determined to make a success of life as his young country, he should be alright.

Prešeren Square

Ljubljana, 2008

You probably haven't heard of France Prešeren; I don't suppose many people have, outside of Slovenia. In Ljubljana, the main square is named after him and his statue stands at its centre, a book tucked under his arm. Here, sunlight flicks over terracotta rooftops and whitewashed walls, art nouveau mingling with baroque as the little river Ljubljanica trickles lazily by.

Prešeren's life spanned just forty-nine years, coinciding with the first half of the nineteenth-century, and only one volume of work was published in his lifetime, but he continues to be a central figure in Slovene culture. There is a national holiday in his honour, marking his death on February 8th, and it was his words that were adopted and set to music when the new republic suddenly found itself in need of a national anthem in 1991.

As very often with iconic poets, Prešeren's legacy seems to be built around personal mythology as much as the poetry itself: he was a melancholy character, a drunkard and philanderer with a turbulent private life involving unrequited love and subsequent depression, and the fathering of three children out of wedlock. The parallels with Dylan Thomas, the 'national poet' who appears on beer-mats in my own small country, and a host of other celebrated poets elsewhere, leaves me wondering what it is about the lives of writers which attracts us to them. It is their myths we are attracted to; the stories of their miseries and misdemeanours that captivate us as we follow the heritage trail.

Maybe it is the chasm that exists between the ideals of their poetry and their failings as human beings that produces in us a kind of melancholy that is, in itself, poetic. Or maybe it's a projection of our own feelings and trivialities onto these rare spirits, a way of making the personal seem universal. Certainly in Prešeren's case, his works in a minority language helped to shape a literature and culture; with Thomas, almost the opposite is true: writing in English he represented a version of Wales to the world. This kind of romanticising is surely more about *us* than *them*. Prešeren and Thomas didn't seek statues or prizes named after them. These things are our ways – in Slovenia and Wales and all small countries – of saying 'Look, he was one of us; if he existed, and felt, so we exist, and feel'.

The only problem is that sometimes in remembering the men and their myths, we forget what it was they were trying to say.

Hostel Celica

Ljubljana, 2008

Ljubljana is sold to travellers as a smaller, friendlier alternative to the jewels of Central Europe. Where Prague is overrun with stag parties in search of cheap beer, Vienna with middle-aged couples in search of Mozart and everybody has at least *heard of* Budapest, Ljubljana has found itself branded as one of a new generation of city break locations for the younger, savvier element of the Easyjet generation.

When I first mentioned to a well-travelled friend that I was thinking of visiting Slovenia, he immediately recommended the Hostel Celica. A former prison reinvented as a backpacker hostel did not immediately seem the ideal place to take my then seven-year-old son, even if its apparently bohemian charms appealed to me. There was no need to worry. Arriving at the city's grey, grotty train station, replete with aggressive dog-wielding beggars and looming communist-era concrete tower blocks, there could be no doubt of our being east of where the Iron Curtain had been raised. But initial doubts quickly gave way to restored faith in humanity as an elderly local helped us, poring over the tiny map in our Lonely Planet guide and leading us across a couple of slushy main roads toward the hostel while muttering to himself and thereby correcting my pronunciation of 'Celica' (both 'c's are rendered 'ch').

From the outside, Celica seems to typify how Westerners imagine the former Eastern Bloc, but its history stretches further back than its use as military barracks by the Yugoslav Federal Army before their defeat in the ten day war of independence in 1991. The building began life as a prison of the Austro-Hungarian Empire in 1883. Surrounded by empty car parks and graffiti the hostel still looks forbidding enough. But once inside, everything seemed familiar, and – like a lot of things in Slovenia – somehow sweet. We were welcomed by a talented band of local schoolchildren – violin, keys, sax, guitar and drums – playing English language rock classics. Moving between proud parents filming the event on cameraphones I slunk to the bar and ordered a non-globalised *Cocka* cola and enjoyed moving renditions of 'Smoke on the Water', 'Should I Stay or Should I Go?' and 'Sweet Child O' Mine' with a ten-year-old Slovene girl on lead vocals.

The whole place – an arts and cultural centre combined with the now semi-famous hostel where you can sleep in the cells – was the result of a ten year struggle, ironic when you consider the brevity of the independence war. A network of artists calling themselves *Metelkova* proposed the idea, then later physically protected the building from demolition before squatting there, enduring deliberate power-cuts perpetrated by the city before eventually being given the go-ahead to collaborate to turn the barracks into an open, welcoming place and a crossroads for travellers.

As we explored the country over the following few days, this initial tableau seemed to be Slovenia in microcosm: a quaint mix of the familiar and the strange, a land partly of the present and partly of the past, precariously poised on the edge of the future.

Next to Celica is the Slovene Ethnographic Museum, a sleek postmodern annex to a grand old building. It houses collections of Slovene artefacts exhibited according to theme and set in context by intelligent and thought-provoking reflections on some of the biggest questions of 'ethnicity'. *Who am I? Who are we?* ponders a giant screen projection against a backdrop of maps and images of this small, beautiful country. There is an exhibition tracing the history of music in Slovenia, its importance as means of ritual and merrymaking at feasts, from the earliest jaw-bone flutes found in caves to the influence of traditional polska, taken by emigrants to America and used as the music of twentieth-century cartoons. The impression is of a young country with an old head on its shoulders.

Back at Celica, twenty-something travellers surf the net over a dodgy connection, local youths drink *Cocka* and play pool, middle-aged provincials wander looking at the art.

And a young Welshman feels strangely at home.

What Everything
Looks Like From Here

Krakow, 2016

As our minibus pulls away from the remains of the camp at Auschwitz-Birkenau into the relative normality of the nondescript south Polish town of Oswiecim, our driver, Konrad, clears his throat. 'In the light of recent events around the world,' he says, his voice catching as it loses the hushed cloak of reverence that has shrouded the entire day at this horrendous place, 'I would like to say two things: please remember that words have meaning, and that these were German death camps.' It's an understandable urge – for a country that was occupied by the Nazis and 'liberated' by the Soviets – to distance innocent Oswiecim from the stain its Germanic corruption has left on human history.

Earlier, we had stood in front of the infamous gates, before the bitter sarcasm of the lie, 'Arbeit Macht Frei'. Our guide, Agnieszka, asks how many glasses wearers are among us. Along with four or five others, I raise my hand. In a group numbering over thirty, I'm surprised how few we are. I see where this is going. What Agnieszka wants us to understand is that Auschwitz did not begin as a death camp for Jews, but as a concentration camp for Polish intellectuals. 'When the Nazis conquered Poland, first they needed to rid the country of anybody who might inspire the minds of the remaining population: teachers, lawyers, doctors, lecturers; they wanted to enslave Poles, and the first step was to imprison the intelligentsia.'

Later, we silently file past piles of shoes and hair belonging to 14,000 exterminated Jewish women; they attest to unspeakable human suffering. No less tragic are the thousands of wire-rimmed spectacles that speak of the eradication of those who today might be termed 'the liberal elite'.

Like Konrad said, words have meaning; words matter. 'Liberal elite' is a collocation that needs prising apart if the rise of fascism is to be smashed in our own time. Quite simply, there is no reason to equate liberalism with elitism. Behind such lazy shorthand lies the same dangerous impulse that targets the intelligentsia or the Jew. The wish to discredit the social position of those who defend human rights or freedom of speech, or who have a healthy regard for values like equality is the same logic that locks up journalists and professors as enemies of the state. The first casualties of war are the truth and its proponents, and fascism does not wait for the pretext of war before it begins taking prisoners.

I have, as a teacher, visited Sachsenhausen and Dachau, outside Berlin and Munich respectively; these camps were the Nazis' early experiments in the concentration and death camps which were to pockmark the whole continent of Europe in the first half of the 1940s. On those occasions, I was stunned into a horrified silence, a prolonged and intensified version of the kind reserved for those two minutes in November when you force yourself to stand stock still and, full of British reserve and stiff upper lip, try and fail to imagine the horrors of Passchendaele and Gallipoli, Stalingrad, Coventry and Dresden. But here at Auschwitz, I didn't feel much like remaining silent.

The very last reaction I want to have is to keep my dignity. There is no dignity in such disregard for humanity. I don't feel different here because I am not on a school trip, but am here with my own son; I don't feel different because I have visited other camps before, or because Auschwitz-Birkenau remains by far the most infamous instrument of the Shoah. I feel different because this is now.

Within days of taking office, the President of the United States of America, the so-called 'land of the free', signed an executive order to allow the torture of human beings, followed by another to ban human beings from seven Muslim majority countries from entering the United States. Regardless of who they are as individuals, it is their nationality, race and religion that will define and demonise them in the eyes of the security services.

Words have meaning. According to Agnieszka, Pastor Martin Niemoller's famous quotation, much repeated in recent days, might have begun, 'First they came for the glasses wearers...' Well, this glasses wearer is not a Muslim, but if the fascists of this generation are coming for the Muslims first, then it's my Christian duty and my human duty to stand with Muslims everywhere, just as I would stand with Jews or Gentiles, socialists or conservatives, gays or straights, if they faced the same persecution. Surely this time *they will not pass*? Words have meaning alright. As a glasses wearer, the only weapon in my hand is a pen – but this machine kills fascists.

Probably the Best
Country in the World

Ebeltoft, 2017

Djursland markets itself as 'the wildest part of Denmark', and yet even in its remotest corners there is something pristine about it. A Best Kept Village competition would be surplus to requirements here; there is, it seems, no necessity to incentivise cleanliness. In village after village and town after town, red-brick houses with inverted V-shaped roofs like those in children's drawings cluster against a backdrop of evergreen trees and wild, changeable skies, neatly protected by perfectly trimmed hedgerows and well-tended flowerbeds. Denmark is a land of superlatives, and the happiest country on earth is perhaps also the tidiest.

The utopian atmosphere seems to extend to everything, including the endless daylight hours. It is summer, which of course makes everything better, but I imagine that given Christmas lights, Scandi knitwear, the national obsession with interior design and everything I half-understand about the in-vogue concept of *hygge*, the Danes are pretty contented in the endless dark of the winter too. *Hygge* is one of those untranslatable concepts that most languages aspire to contain; the English word 'cosy' clearly does not cover all of the use of *hygge* and its variant adjective *hyggelig*. According to the brochure, Ebeltoft is a 'cosy market town' where you can do some 'cosy shopping' and have a 'cosy time' purchasing all manner of cosy objects to make you feel cosy.

There is something, of course, in the Danes' desire to feel cosy

– to light candles, to furnish their homes with tactile fabrics – pitted as they are for most of the year against the cold and the dark. But it's not only the design-led shaping of the physical environment for which Danes are internationally famed. Denmark's reputation as a social utopia is unmatched even by its neighbours across the Baltic Sea, which all also rank highly both in the happiness leagues, both in the global imagination and in the cold hard facts of scientific study. Finland (Best Education System in the World™), Sweden (Best Country in the World to be an Immigrant and top of the Good Country Index) and Norway (overtaking Denmark in the 2017 Happiness Index) all take some beating, but the Danes often come first among equals, not that they like to brag.

Scotland, particularly with its moves toward independence, makes increasingly explicit overtures about Nordic models and Scandinavian social systems. These high tax, high welfare economies, perhaps because of a perception of a prevailing gentle liberalism, escape the criticisms that might come if an economy like the UK's began to implement the kind of radical social engineering that has, over generations, reduced inequality and improved quality of life to the extent that Denmark has become, to borrow the slogan of its signature lager, probably the best country in the world.

Denmark does have a dark side, of course. *Hamlet* didn't exactly end well, or start well for that matter. Likewise *The Killing*. And the fairytales of Hans Christian Andersen don't always match up to their Disneyfication. But the overwhelming impression of this remarkable little nation is one that is more than validated here. Peaceful, prosperous and progressive; crystal clear waters, endless summer evenings and a gentle breeze through meadows of wildflowers. What's not to like?

The Boundless Kitchen

Ebeltoft, 2017

The girl steps up to the microphone again. She moves like a star, all sideways glances, gentle swaying of the hips and nonchalant flicks of her long dark hair. She is about nine years old.

Having already performed one song with conviction, she is about to deliver another. But nobody was expecting *this*. The first number had been a Kurdish folk song, albeit backed with pop chords from an electronic keyboard. Now, emboldened by the presence of a boy – brother, cousin or friend – the girl launches passionately into the ubiquitous global hit of the summer.

Mostly in Spanish with brief explosions of English, the magic of 'Despacito' here lies in the fact that it's sung by two Syrian-Kurdish kids to a predominantly Danish audience. Diversity here extends to differences as miniscule as the exact shape of one's wire-rimmed spectacles, the patterns on silk scarves and a spectrum of hair colours that stretches from golden sun-blonde to whitish moon-silver through every conceivable shade of grey.

Nordic people are nice, polite, reserved, radiating a gentle warmth without the effusion of flame. Here at *Det Grænseløse Køkken* (the Boundless Kitchen), a large purpose-built structure and glass housing long communal tables, it is as if the recent wave of immigration (part of the fallout of Europe's refugee crisis) has lit a cultural touchpaper. Artistic conception and promotional notes can only hint at the mystery of what really happens when cultures meet.

'Around the world, the process of gathering to share a meal is a social instinct based on love, mutuality and friendship,' says the promotional blurb for the 'communal eating events' that will take place in Ebeltoft, the nearby city of Aarhus and elsewhere throughout 2017. 'The meal and the creation of it can be used as a social tool to break down cultural barriers,' the publicity materials continue. But to taste the meal – to dig out spiced bulgur wheat from inside grilled red bell-peppers; to bite into soft stuffed vine leaves, to mop up thick clods of hummus sprinkled with jewel-like pomegranate seeds using half-moon shaped paper-thin flatbreads is to experience something of the lives of others.

Shakespeare used food and music as metaphors for each other and, of course, illustrations of love. And, of course, he was right. After we've queued again for generous second-helpings and had our icy northern European social barriers not so much broken down but melted, the music strikes up. This being summer in Denmark, there is no chance yet of the sun beginning to dip. It is still some hours before the purplish light will fade into an indigo semi-darkness that will linger briefly before giving way to an early dawn, but the effect of the music is the same.

Immediately the long-necked *tembur*, the Kurdish eqivalent of the *oud*, strikes up and we are transported to the Middle East on the wailing cry of the singer. Knowing what we know, it may be tempting to poeticise the melancholia of the music, to imagine these songs as lamentations for a lost homeland, reflections on the pain of exile.

Like perhaps all folk musics, even without any understanding of the lyric, the song communicates both passion and pain. This being Kurdish folk music, and – particularly now – Syrian-Kurdish folk music, there is a high likelihood that this is about the pain of separation from home. And yet, watching the singer watching the two youngsters who follow him (he may or may not be the father of one or both), it is easy to focus not on what has been lost and what must be mourned, but on what future lies in store. These beautiful dark-featured children will grow up – are already growing up – in Denmark, the happiest country in the world.

It is hard to know how long they might have been here, but Mohammed, the Syrian-Kurdish cook who was introduced to us before the meal, seemed to speak decent Danish, and the Syrian war has been raging for six long years. It is conceivable that these kids don't remember Syria; in some ways, I hope they don't.

And 'Despacito' is not an incongruous choice. Syrian-Kurdish refugee children singing a Puerto Rican-Canadian collaboration before an audience of Danes, plus Brits, Australians, Germans and assorted others. Increasingly, it will only be writers and cultural commentators who are concerned with distinctions of genre or language based on ethnic origin or nationality. For these kids, they are simply singing a song they like.

This summer 'Despacito' has had three billion plays on YouTube. This fact alone tells us it's a song that transcends language and culture; it belongs to everyone and no one. Marshall McLuhan was a prophet from the last century; we've been living in a global village for a while now. Those of us in wire-rimmed spectacles, sipping bottled beers while tapping our toes, may have read about it in newspaper supplements or understood the documentaries. But these kids, Kurdish-Danes, belting out 'Despacito' before running off to play in treehouses, they're living it.

Living Danishly

Aarhus, 2017

Of all the trips I have taken, this was the one I had perhaps looked forward to least. It wasn't only the fact I had been turned down for a job that I had counted my chickens on a few days before we set off, or the prospect of six solid days of heavy rain, broken up with the treat of one cloudy day (which is what the Weather App had forecast); it was also possibly because the idea of going to rural Jutland was, in the first place, a bit random.

If we had been heading to Copenhagen, our destination would at least have made sense. Couples in their mid-thirties are often off on weekend breaks to places like Copenhagen (i.e. capital cities of smaller European nations with readymade tourist infrastructure). Sure, we had the perfect cover story in that Aarhus, Denmark's second city, situated on the east coast of central Jutland – the country's main peninsula that literally juts out into the Baltic Sea – was European Capital of Culture 2017 and therefore hosting a panoply of exhibitions and events. But we weren't exactly staying in Aarhus, although the nearest airport is named for it.

A forty-five minute drive from Aarhus, Ebeltoft (literally: apple-land) is a small market town situated on the edge of a sweeping bay and the Mols-Bjerge National Park. As well as being a sleepy little coastal town, popular in season with German tourists and native Danes who have second homes here, it is the unlikely home of the European Film College – which is, courtesy of a friend who teaches there, where we are staying.

The college is an exercise in Danishness, a perfect introduction to the country if you like your pre-existing stereotypes confirmed. The college juxtaposes the architectural modernity of clean lines, whitewashed concrete and glass with a backwoodsy natural setting that nevertheless feels very safe and civilised. Whereas I imagine the forests of northern Sweden and Finland and the icy fjords of Norway are verging on genuinely inhospitable wildernesses, here in southern Scandinavia it seems you are afforded the perfect blend of interior comfort and outdoor natural beauty.

The Danes, world-famous for their stylish interior design with its emphasis on ergonomic shapes, natural materials and perfect intricate lighting arrangements, seem to have mastered the balance between indoors and out. No wonder, perhaps, that in survey after survey, Denmark is declared the happiest country in the world.

I'd guess it is all down to the seasons. Where the natural world presents civilisation with its greatest challenges, mankind is forced to come up with the tidiest solutions. In Britain, where the intermittent environmental challenges are kind of low-key, we manage to do what we are best at: muddling through. Meanwhile, the Danes get on with producing a third of their energy from wind power, harnessing and working with the elements to efficiently provide clean, green solutions. They are aiming for 100% of electricity production to come from wind by 2050, and I'm pretty sure they'll achieve it.

Within hours of being in Ebeltoft, we have slowed. The speed restrictions on Denmark's roads, coupled with the fact that maximums are given in kilometres, serving to further round down expected limits, mean that we can't do much else while driving. But our walking has slowed too, almost naturally. There is some of the effect of heightened senses you get in any foreign environment, accentuated further perhaps by the fact that flora and fauna are little different to Britain.

The path from the film college down into Ebeltoft is flanked by wildflower meadows – long yellowing grasses, thistles, dandelions –

and thick hedgerows packed with pine cones and orange-red berries. The primacy of evergreen provides a wintry feel to the bright summer's day. Birds sing and crickets chirp but the air retains the crisp, clean, clear quality of a perennially cold climate.

Playgrounds are empty. It is the summer holidays. But the abandoned facilities of a Danish primary school betray the country's emphasis on rearing children with outdoor play and discovery, and the high taxes which fund an excellent state system that supports the happiest children in the world. Rope swings in the woods, treehouses, rows of high quality wooden play cabins, ample parking space for bicycles: all seem to be the norm here. Through the gaps in well-maintained fences, a glimpse of just one or two white-blonde six-year-olds playing in the woods, independently but within shouting distance of an ever-vigilant adult, is tableau enough of childhood idyll to make living Danishly an aim to which any sane person would want to aspire.

As we walk further past a very quiet leisure centre and a small gym, we talk of how our own quality of life indicators could be improved, and where we might move in our own country to give our children a more Danish upbringing. We understand that Denmark cannot possibly be perfect, but on a few days' evidence there do seem to be an inordinate number of things this nation of just 5.5 million people is getting right. A week in a country without sight of a single piece of litter or evidence of petty vandalism and where people routinely leave expensive bicycles to stand unlocked must have something about it.

Living Danishly is about work-life balance and living with, rather than against, the natural environment; about buying quality that lasts rather than supporting a throwaway culture that spawns a dearth of quality goods and a surplus of charity shops. And yes, of course, it's about *hygge*.

Walden Pond

Pontcanna Fields, 2010

Walden Pond, near Concord, Massachusetts was the place chosen by Henry David Thoreau for his experiment in living which tapped into the ancient tradition of hermit-philosopher but that was also a deeply American experience. Thoreau claims it was an 'accident' that his two years of 'Life in the Woods' began on the 4th of July, but Independence Day 1845 seems a fitting date to have begun a great American adventure. As a critic has noted, Walden is not only the story of a man who goes to live in the woods, 'it is also the story of a man who built a house.'

For here is not – as the book is often billed – an account of a man giving up on society, or even rebelling against it. Thoreau comes across as a thinker who believes deeply in a balance between company and solitude. He is also a master of the extended metaphor: 'Time is but the stream I go a-fishing in. I drink at it; but while I drink I see the sandy bottom and detect how shallow it is. Its thin current slides away, but eternity remains. I would drink deeper; fish in the sky, whose bottom is pebbly with stars.' Thoreau believed in the intellect as 'a cleaver' and his head as 'an organ for burrowing... a divining rod' and Walden was the place he chose to 'mine'.

He believed in education too, and in books. Perhaps surprisingly for a man who has gone to live in the woods, his concern is as much with worthwhile reading as much as it is with catching fish. As much as anything, Thoreau went to Walden so that he could concentrate on Plato without the distraction of newspapers. A broadband connection would probably not have been on his list of basic requirements if he were to repeat the experiment today.

What Thoreau realised was that so much of life is a distraction from what really matters. He wanted to live, to approach the essence of things. Modern America, using Thoreau as a touchstone, would do well to remember his own points of reference throughout the work, which frequently include Confucius and the *Bhagavad Gita*. But also his defence of 'We Americans and moderns generally'. He attacks those who are 'dinning in our ears' that Americans – being the population of a young country – are 'intellectual dwarfs compared to the ancients, or even the Elizabethan[s]' by making the very American claim that 'A living dog is better than a dead lion.'

Thoreau is a champion of life and the living. And yes, he is a champion of the individual: 'If a man does not keep pace with his companions, maybe it is because he hears a different drummer.' America's mid-nineteenth-century transcendentalists are full of such wisdom, much of it drawn from the waters of Walden, which Thoreau calls 'my well ready dug'.

City Lights

San Francisco, 2008

San Francisco is one of the world's truly great cities; there is no doubt about that. It is me I worry about. After an epic drive up Highway 1, all the way from San Diego and the Mexican border, what kind of person shuns the Golden Gate Bridge, Pier 39, the dubious delights of Alcatraz and even the flower power generation's countercultural hub of Haight-Ashbury for a medium-sized independent bookstore? I've even brought with me one of those special edition Moleskine notebooks with a blue biro cross marking the corner building on Columbus Avenue where San Francisco's (*never* call it 'Frisco') historic Chinatown meets the Italian-dominated North Beach area.

City Lights, of course, is no ordinary bookshop. Founded by Lawrence Ferlinghetti and Peter D. Martin in 1953, the store was originally the latter's idea. He had first used the *City Lights* name – in homage to the Chaplin film – for a magazine, to which Ferlinghetti contributed poems under the name Lawrence Ferling. When Martin decided to open America's first all-paperback bookshop, Ferlinghetti introduced himself and the rest is history. Originally, the shop was a partnership, with each man stumping up five hundred dollars. Two years in, Martin upped sticks to New York, selling the business to Ferlinghetti, who has been there ever since.

At ground level, the store resembles many other independent bookstores: it has shelves, with books on. I think somewhere at the back of my mind I was expecting Ginsberg standing on a table ranting about Buddha, Kerouac passing a joint around and Bobby Dylan busking outside, throwing lyrics on the floor like he does in the video for 'Subterranean Homesick Blues'. Instead, there is a placard propped in a corner with the slogan *FREE THE PRESS* (in brackets beneath it says *from its corporate owners*, in case we wondered) but otherwise the ambience of the shop feels quite, well, *corporate*. The tills are manned by hipsters in City Lights T-shirts but they don't look 'angelheaded'. I can't imagine them 'dragging themselves through the negro streets at dawn looking for an angry fix'; they look more like the Starbucks type. There are City Lights posters and City Lights postcards. It is a shop, after all.

In the basement, the feel is slightly more bohemian; stacks of books balanced on and against long wooden planks. City Lights specialises in world literature, the arts and progressive politics. Most of the books you might not find in Waterstones are down here. I find an old copy of Ferlinghetti's best-known work *A Coney Island of the Mind*; it feels wrong not to buy it. City Lights is an imprint too – the famous Pocket Poets series was the first to publish Ginsberg's 'Howl' – which became embroiled in an obscenity trial ending with Judge Clayton Horn's decision that the poem was far from being obscene but of 'redeeming social importance'.

I browse the shelves dedicated to what is still one of America's most exciting poetry presses and pick up a volume of Pablo Neruda Ferlinghetti put out to celebrate the centenary of the Chilean Nobel laureate. It presents the Spanish originals alongside the translations; I mutter a few words of the Spanish to myself. It sounds beautiful, though I don't understand it fully without the translation. 'I love your wide-open poetry,' Neruda told Ferlinghetti as both poets waited among the Fidelistas in Havana after the Cuban Revolution. Ferlinghetti's response: 'You opened the door.'

I open the door to the small room upstairs at City Lights, next to where Ferlinghetti, now ninety, has his office. Its door is adorned with a mock Parisian street sign: 'NOT PLACE ST

GERMAIN DES PRES'. This is the famous poetry room, where once the Beats held forth amid clouds of dope smoke. There was, just like in Greenwich Village on the other side of America, 'music in the cafés at night and revolution in the air'. Now the room feels strangely, almost exceptionally, empty.

There are framed photographs on the wall, Larry Keenan's famous black and white shots of an occasion they call 'The Last Gathering of Beat Poets and Artists'. Ferlinghetti, ever the organiser, had wanted to document the San Francisco scene in 1965 in the spirit of the classic early twentieth-century photographs of the bohemian artists and writers of Paris. All the usual suspects are there. Most of them, like so many other notables of their generation, died too soon. Even by this point, many had, as Ginsberg wrote, had 'their minds destroyed by madness'. The kind of freedom they hinted at in their 'wide-open poetry' was soon trampled over by the consumer society.

Back downstairs I join the bohemian masses buying postcards: Kerouac with Neal Cassady and again on the beach in Tangier with Peter Orlovsky and William Burroughs, and a poster showing City Lights in the fifties. I'm a literary tourist, a lifestyle consumer. Of course a bookshop can't change the world. What it can do, of course, is offer a meeting place for exchanging ideas. That has been the importance of City Lights over the years.

On my way out I spot a cut-price audiobook. It's called *Dreams From My Father,* the autobiography of Barack Obama, the Illinois senator challenging Hillary Clinton for the Democratic Presidential nomination. Alongside Bob Dylan's *Desire* it becomes the soundtrack to the rest of the road trip. On up the coast to the giant Redwoods, through the forest fires sweeping northern California and then down through the stark beauty of the Sierra Nevada and back across the Mojave to Los Angeles on Route 66, I listen to this calm voice of intelligence and compassion and once again am filled with hope, for America and for the world.

Hollywood Forever

Los Angeles, 2008

The Westwood Village Memorial Park Cemetery is famous for housing the interred remains of Marilyn Monroe. As such, it is one of the most popular celebrity grave pilgrimages in the world, rivalled only by the eclectic likes of Shakespeare and Princess Diana, Jim Morrison and Elvis, Mark Twain and Oscar Wilde. But this quiet cemetery, hidden away in this upmarket suburb of Los Angeles, is also the final resting place of many other stars of stage, screen and letters. Dean Martin, Truman Capote and Jack Lemmon – whose headstone reads simply 'Jack Lemmon in', comically indicating the ground – all have their final resting place here.

But in terms of memorable epitaphs, there is none better than Marilyn and Jack's director on *Some Like It Hot*, Billy Wilder. Using a play on the film's famous last scene, in which Jerry (Lemmon) takes off his wig to reveal that he can't marry Osgood (Joe E. Brown) because 'I'm a man!' to which he gets the immortal reply, 'Well, nobody's perfect.'

It seems fitting that the director had the good humour to ally the comic line that cemented his place in movie history with the fact of being 'a writer'. It also shows that despite his skills as an auteur, Billy Wilder considered himself, first and foremost, a writer. Unlike his more experimental contemporaries like Hitchcock and Welles, who were reinventing cinema with films like *Psycho* and *Citizen Kane*, Wilder was a storyteller. His conservative cinematography allowed for tightly scripted character-driven plots and in the process produced some of the most memorable films of Hollywood's Golden Age.

Even if you haven't seen the films, titles like *Sunset Boulevard* and *Double Indemnity* are redolent of an almost mythical era when the film industry seem to capture America in her mid twentieth-century pomp. *Indemnity* was his collaboration with Raymond Chandler and for many the apotheosis of film noir. *Sunset Boulevard*, as its title suggests, is about Hollywood itself. The main character, Joe Gillis, played by William Holden, is a screenwriter. He sums up his film-writing career with the remark, 'The last one I wrote was about Okies in the dustbowl. You'd never know, because when it reached the screen, the whole thing played on a torpedo boat.' When another character says 'I'd always heard that you had some talent', he replies, 'That was last year. This year I'm trying to make a living.'

Other writers may have been more caustic in their criticism of the censorship laws, but few were as successful as Wilder in pushing the boundaries back. His films – *The Lost Weekend*, an adaptation of Charles R. Jackson's story about alcoholism and *The Apartment* and *The Seven-Year Itch* about infidelity and adultery – defied the censors and put real life issues on screen for the first time.

What Wilder realised about characters – and therefore about people in general – now glints in gold in the west coast sunlight. The inscription on his headstone reinforces the fact that far from being a throwaway remark the line is an insight into the human condition that all true writers know only too well: Nobody's Perfect.

Kerala: Making Hay
in God's Own Country

Trivandrum, 2011

Thiruvananthapuram, capital city of the state of Kerala, in the far south-west of India, is as crowded with people as its name is with syllables. By mid-November, most of the monsoon rains have passed and the city is bathed in a stiflingly sticky wet heat. The main thoroughfare, Mahatma Gandhi Road – a statue of the great man stands at an intersection garlanded with orange and yellow flowers – is a constant cacophony of traffic. Swarms of black and yellow rickshaws buzz like so many bees amid the jumble of modern cars, motorbikes, scooters and 1950s classics. Cracked, worn and nonexistent pavements overflow with women in bejewelled saris of pink and red and green while shirtless young men bedecked in beads, hands on each others' shoulders in a chain of Hindu brotherhood, make their way joyfully to worship at Sree Padmanabhaswamy, home to a treasure-house of gold that makes it the world's richest temple.

Crowds and noise are Indian leitmotifs. When, during the opening ceremony of the second annual Hay Festival in Kerala, bare-chested drummers compete with the paparazzi photographers surrounding Shashi Tharoor – writer, critic, member of parliament for Kerala and one-time nominee for the post of UN Secretary General – an English publisher, who has lived in Kerala for the last decade, leans over to me and says: 'In India, if it isn't crowded and it isn't noisy, then nothing's happening.'

Something is certainly happening here. Kanakakunnu Palace, where the local maharaja once entertained the British Raj, is situated on a hill near the city's museum, art gallery and zoo. It is an oasis of relative calm. But the multicoloured banners tied between trees and tents in the garden and the purple and silver bunting that shimmers in the breeze marks the fact that Hay has arrived. Kerala's near-100% literacy rate, a legacy of one of the world's first democratically elected communist governments, is the envy of all India and despite that a short walk confirms that we are very much still in a developing country here, Thiruvananthapuram does seem the perfect place for the festival's Indian incarnation.

The success story of the original literary festival, in Hay on Wye (Arthur Miller: 'Is that some kind of sandwich?') is fairly well known. Aside from Miller's witticism, the most famous line about the festival belongs to Bill Clinton, who on his visit to the Welsh capital of secondhand books in 2001 called it 'The Woodstock of the Mind.' Perhaps less well known – at least in Britain – is Hay's rapid expansion as a global phenomenon. Peter Florence and his team now run festivals from Merthyr Tydfil to the Maldives, from Belfast to Beirut and from Segovia in Spain to Xalapa in Mexico. Kerala seems an entirely appropriate setting for the kind of cultural exchange exported by Hay. Festival co-director Lyndy Cooke admits that this one is her favourite.

There are a billion people in the world's only country to occupy what we have come to call 'the subcontinent'. A billion people make a billion Indias. But despite the multiplicity – of languages, of religions, of caste, of colour, of politics – there are national characteristics. That, among many other things, is what Hay Festivals are good at. There is a careful curation at work in creating a programme of events that present a plurality of voices; the result is a coherent, if complex snapshot of literary India today. This is a country poised on the crest of a huge wave of economic boom and rapid change, so perhaps unsurprisingly, pluralism and complexity emerge as the themes of the festival. For me, the highlight of the three days is a session where the local festival director, the irrepressibly genial Sanjoy Roy, speaks to Tarun Tejpal, the Indian novelist and editor of *Tehelka*. Or rather, is spoken to. As Roy readily admits afterward, 'All you have to do is press play.'

Tejpal is no shrinking violet. In a conversation ostensibly about his bestselling novels, *The Alchemy of Desire* and *Story of my Assassins*, the writer often shoots off on violent trajectories that offer an excoriating analysis of India today. If there are parallels between Shining India and Great Britain in her Victorian pomp – the 'bubble' lived in by the rich, the mindboggling levels of social and economic inequality, the extent to which society is riddled with both petty and large-scale corruption – then Tejpal is its Dickens. Himself a member of the privileged class, the novelist and editor stands up for the kid born 'the wrong side of the tracks'.

He describes his novel *The Alchemy of Desire* as 'the counternarrative of India – the story of the underclass.' All of his writing, he admits, is pervaded by a love of his country: 'India is the only thing that interests me. This is the best place to be a writer,' he claims, 'the best place to be a journalist. This country is in foment. It's the future of the world, but it's founded on complexities.' One of Tejpal's many concerns is that the new, so-called 'Shining' India is forgetting the principles of the 'founding fathers'. Nehru's constitution is under threat from anti-corruption legislation, but the novelist is slow to condemn all forms of corruption out of hand; the picture is more complicated than that. 'For the kid born in the slums of Calcutta or Mumbai, corruption is one of the few weapons available to make one's way in the world.'

This kind of complexity is at the heart of India's language problem too. Whether riding in rickshaws around the town, or being served canapés of spiced chicken and fish in five star hotels on the beachfront, it is clear that for the ordinary Indian, English is the *lingua franca* rather than a literary language. The level of spoken English varies greatly. The poet and translator Arvind Krishna Mehrotra is bold enough to put his finger on the problem.

In a session titled 'Twice-told Fictions: The New Life of Translations', toward the end of a discussion between poets, novelists, translators and publishers, Mehrotra says: 'Why don't we admit that sometimes the English we write makes no bloody sense?' Wordy pontificating, I am learning, is not an Indian trait.

On the other hand, despite the international nature of the festival – with star turns from Germaine Greer, Jung Chang and Simon Armitage among others – and the many languages spoken, including a memorable 'mash up' poetry session with writers in English, Welsh, Hindi, Bengali and Malayalam all riffing off each others' work in a beautiful soundclash of cultures, the English spoken at the festival is exemplary. If anything, the eloquence of both words and ideas expressed at this relatively cosy meeting of minds points the direction for the future of the English-speaking world. Like India itself, English-language literature is polyphonic, multicultural, fragmentary and complicated. And all the better for it.

As the time nears to leave this big, beautiful, bewildering country – the last night's party is followed by a paddle in the warm waters of the Arabian sea, beneath a coconut-tree sky – I feel privileged not only to have shared in its riches, the tropical climate, the abundance of flora and fauna, the exotic wildlife, the wonderful food, but also to have glimpsed its cultural treasures.

The annual pilgrimage to Hay-on-Wye has long been part of the British booklovers' calendar. Tony Benn spoke for many when he said, 'In my mind it has replaced Christmas.' The Whitsun bank holiday is one of the few weekends of the year when I know, barring very exceptional circumstances, exactly where I will be. But Hay in Hay has been teetering on the brink of being a victim of its own success; like Glastonbury or the Edinburgh Fringe, it has almost become so big as to have necessarily forgotten some of what made it so charmingly exhilarating in the first place. Hay's move into the global arena is a smart move in every sense. After Kerala, the team are moving on to Dhaka to pilot a festival in Bangladesh. Within hours, Peter Florence is tweeting that this new baby has 'catapulted into the premier league'. The whole thing is clearly a labour of love. By starting all over again, in places where the concept of a festival of literature and ideas is entirely new, Hay is constantly refreshing itself by recapturing the spirit that made it such an organic success in the first place. Malayalam novelist M. Mukundan inadvertently summed up the Hay philosophy when talking about literature in general in the very first session: 'Reach out to the world.'

At the back of my notebook there is a small library of books I have promised to read when I get home, most of them recommended by Arvind Mehrotra. Small scratches on the surface of the subcontinent they may be, but to scratch the surface in Kerala was not only to glimpse the gold of 'God's Own Country', but also to leave with dirt under my fingernails, the scent of which I hope will linger for a long, long time to come.

Mexico: Dying for the Truth

Mexico City, 2015

Yes, these are sad and crazy times for Mexico. It is a country that is a victim of corruption, US drug consumption and amoral gun selling, poverty, human trafficking, and where the constant killing of journalists means that the storyteller has become the story. But we cannot think that this, that seems so specific, is Mexico. No. This is the world we are all living in.

Jennifer Clements, President of PEN International; former President of PEN Mexico

The titles alone tell a story. *Mexico: Narco-Violence and a Failed State?*; *Drug War Mexico: Politics, Neoliberalism and Violence in the New Narcoeconomy*; *Narcoland: The Mexican Drug Lords and Their Godfathers*; *Mexico: Democracy Interrupted*. On top of the alarming reports issued by PEN International in advance of the freedom-of-speech organisation's third delegation to Mexico in under four years, a scan of recent nonfiction titles about Central America's dominant republic are enough to make this humble delegate from newly-formed Wales PEN Cymru more than a little trepidatious.

On arrival in Mexico City, the most unnerving thing is the sense of normality. As Ioan Grillo notes in *El Narco: The Bloody Rise of*

Mexican Drug Cartels, 'Mexico is an advanced country with a trillion dollar economy, several world-class companies, and eleven billionaires. It has an educated middle class with a quarter of young people going to university. It has some of the best beaches, resorts and museums on the planet.' All of which is eminently evidenced as this megalopolis of more than twenty million people goes about its business amid luxury hotels, the offices of multi-national corporations and – perhaps the ultimate symbol of twenty-first-century Western capitalism – a Starbucks on every corner.

But even here, in the relative safety of downtown, signs are here that something is rotten. Police presence is ubiquitous. My parkland stroll up to the history museum is suddenly accompanied by two truckloads of uniformed troops. Outside a government building near my hotel, an Occupy-style encampment has been set up in protest at the inadequacies of the investigation into the disappearance of forty-three students in Ayotzinapa, Guerrero state, last September. Its ski-masked campaigners are under observation from a police helicopter circling incessantly above. And the first Mexican I speak to – a taxi driver – provides less than two minutes of small talk before he gets around to *la violencia*, *el corrupcion* and a hand gesture that implies *el gobierno* are taking for themselves *mucho dinero* while letting the real problems go untackled.

Jacobo is taking me to Trotsky's house, where the exiled revolutionary met his famed ice-pick-assisted end. Amid the photos and personal effects of the museum is a story of fear, intrigue and brutal execution that would not be out of place in the Mexico of today. However, it is a quiet part of town; Trotsky's garden is a suntrap, and a haven from the gridlock and noise of one of the world's biggest cities. The driver agrees to wait for me, and parks up around the corner for an afternoon nap, a newspaper folded over his face. When I emerge and we set off, he leans out of the window to pay off a policeman who has had the grace to allow him to remain at the roadside. It is the pettiest act, barely worthy of being called corruption. And yet the small-scale nature of Jacobo's indiscretion is indicative of the endemic, systemic nature of Mexico's problem. How, I wonder aloud to journalists the following day, can a citizen be so open about denouncing corruption to a foreigner, only minutes later to undermine his own complaint by openly participating in what is clearly ingrained in the country's culture?

My audience includes Federico Mastrogiovanni, an Italian writer who has lived in Mexico City for six years. His book *Ni Vivos, Ni Muertos* is the inaugural winner of PEN Mexico's prize for investigative journalism. The presentation of awards to such writers as Mastrogiovanni is an important part of a strategy to raise awareness of the situation faced by writers and journalists in Mexico. The Italian collects his prize alongside the director of human rights group Article 19, Dario Ramirez, the journalist Pablo Ferri and the *grande dame* of Mexican letters, Elena Poniatowska, who receives the prize 'for everything'.

PEN International's mission is to promote literature and freedom of expression around the world. The organisation therefore has vast experience of sending delegations of prominent writers to bring international attention and pressure to bear upon questionable regimes. But in recent years Mexico has, for numerous reasons, become a particular focus for PEN, subjected to an unprecedented series of major visits. Partly, this is due to the gravity of the situation: one hundred and three journalists killed since 2000, twenty-five more forcibly disappeared, and with a 90% rate of impunity. It also has something to do with the partial success of previous missions: Enrique Peña Nieto, Mexican president since 2012, has created a constitutional amendment that allows a federal prosecutor to punish crimes against freedom of expression.

However, as became evident throughout my time in Mexico – participating in PEN International's Summit of the Americas and a large public event, PEN Pregunta – the mechanism for implementing this law is not working. One after another, representatives from a range of Mexican NGOs take the floor to outline the problems faced: the lack of professionalism and low wages of local and regional journalists; financial pressures and the lack of protection afforded by media organisations for their own staff; the impossibility of reporting accurately on public demonstrations. Ultimately, however, they all say the same thing: there is a lack of political will to prosecute the murderers of journalists.

The fact that the British state is rolling out the red carpet for the state visit of President Peña Nieto has potential to be deeply worrying. The President and his wife will stay with the Queen and Prince Philip at Buckingham Palace, following Prince Charles' visit to Mexico last November. 2015 is the Dual Year of UK and Mexico 2015, 'a year-long celebration of cultural, educational and business exchange between our two nations'. Among other arts activity, Mexico will be the featured country at the London Book Fair; the Hay Festival will be a partner in the publication of *Mexico 20*, an anthology of writing from a new generation of Mexican authors.

If you check the website, it all looks like a very positive cultural exchange programme. There will be exhibitions, symposia and trade summits. And yet this exchange is happening against a backdrop of what PEN International President John Ralston Saul has called the 'unholy trinity' of corruption, violence and impunity. PEN Pregunta – PEN Asks – was about standing up and asking pertinent questions. One wonders whether the next three days will bring uncomfortable questions for Mr Peña Nieto to answer, or whether the Queen and David Cameron will simply treat the Mexican President as head of another rising economy where there is ample cheap labour and a huge new potential market for British investment.

Djemaa el-Fna

Marrakech, 2014

Of all the world's famous city squares, there can be none quite like the Djemaa el-Fna. Red Square might be home to the Kremlin, St Basil's Cathedral and Lenin's mausoleum as well as memories of Soviet displays of power; St Peter's Square may be a focal point for a billion Catholics; Mexico City's Zocalo may be bigger; London's Trafalgar Square and Buenos Aires' Plaza de Mayo may have taller, more impressive columns and edifices; Tahrir Square over in Cairo may have dominated the headlines during the Arab Spring; but for sheer everyday human drama, not to mention mouth-watering sensory overload, Djemaa el-Fna is unsurpassed.

By day, this irregular-shaped patch of concrete that opens out from the exits and entrances of the labyrinthine souks of Marrakech is thronged with snake charmers, Barbary apes on chains and street-hawkers on the make. By night, it becomes one of the northern hemisphere's most atmospheric open-air restaurants.

In a square lined with cafés, where you can gain temporary respite from the crowds and heat of south-western Morocco over a slow-brewed and cooling mint tea, the culinary choices of evening become perplexing. Smoke from grilled meat and steam from the miniature chimneys of a thousand tagines rise like incense to the gods of north African cuisine, while at ground level the waiters double as the Marrakech equivalent of used-car salesmen.

111

Cheap flights here from all over Europe have rendered these clever businessmen expert in a wide range of languages and cultures. Their knowledge may be shallow, but it is sufficient for its purpose: getting people to sit in their plastic chairs rather than somebody else's. It works on us, anyhow.

'*Bonjour*, hello, good evening... where are you from?' asks our eventual host as we window-shop his falafels.

'Wales,' we say, expecting that he hasn't heard of it.

'Ooh, *siarad Cymraeg*?' he asks, in a not-too-shabby approximation of a slightly camp strain of South Walian Welshiness. '*Gavin and Stacey*? Ryan Giggs? There's lovely...'

'You had us at *siarad Cymraeg*,' I smile. 'Go on, we'll eat here.'

He brings us cutlery, napkins and a basket of bread. There's no wine, for the obvious reason that Djemaa el-Fna is in the shadow of the impressive Koutoubia Mosque, once known as the Bookseller's Mosque for its sheltering of nearly a hundred book vendors in the adjacent souk. Now food for thought has been succeeded by food for the body, even the hordes of Westerners don't mind that there's a juice list instead.

I watch the waiter turn immediately from us in an attempt to engage a passing German couple. '*Guten Abend?*' he says, and I wonder how many greetings and cultural snippets he has at his disposal. A list, no doubt, to rival the choice of fruit juices. What can he tell me about the sitcoms and football heroes of Baden-Wurttemberg, I wonder?

Later, we are offered an opportunity to purchase alcohol, but in order to access the bar we would need to pay the equivalent of around £80 to enter the premises. Such is the cost of a licence in this relatively liberal but still strictly Islamic culture. Rich tourists will no doubt pay for the privilege as well as the seclusion bought by such a premium. For us, despite it being new year's eve, we'd rather sit out on a café roof-terrace overlooking the square and sip mint tea in the night-time chill.

Next to us is a small group of Scandinavians in horn-rimmed

spectacles, all looking earnestly at their watches as midnight approaches. All around, Moroccans chatter on as if it's ten thirty on an average weekday evening. When midnight finally strikes, a few pathetic firecrackers are heard in the distance, an American expat's back garden perhaps. We wish the Scandinavians a muted happy new year and they mutter something back, embarrassed. The locals continue their conversations. Marrakech runs to a different calendar; hours and dates have never felt so arbitrary.

We return to the hotel, stone cold sober and plain stone cold, the chill of an edge-of-desert night-time falling quickly like an interval curtain. Oblivious to our Western travails, the Djemaa el-Fna crackles with life, an everyday Hogmanay.

The Road to Zagora

Sahara Desert, 2014

Zagora is noted because it marks the start of the road to Timbuktu. Fifty-two days, says the sign, referring to the length of time it takes to cross the world's largest desert on foot. The road to Zagora itself is enough adventure for me, especially when it's not been all that long since having watched the film *Taken*, about a violent kidnapping, and its having inspired a recurring dream. As a result, I'm more than a little wary of the excursion-hawkers who throng the evening streets of Marrakech along with the boys selling ornate metalwork candle-lamps for a euro.

But it turns out Gareth Bale is a passport to a discount. For once in Marrakech, the barter is straightforward. We say we're from Wales. He says he loves Real Madrid star Gareth Bale. I say I trained to be a teacher at Whitchurch High School when Bale was in Year 8. He takes a selfie with me for his Facebook profile and tags it 'Le prof de Gareth Bale'. We get a cheap trip to the desert. Our Moroccan Bale-enthusiast circles a busy-looking junction on a map and tells us to wait for a minibus the following morning.

Overnight, I worry that a kidnap is being planned. Informed by my nightmare-on-loop, my overactive imagination tells me that the Facebook selfie was part of an elaborate plot. My wife tells me not to worry but can't stem my overwhelming apprehension. I message a friend in London to tell him where we're going, just in case we're kidnapped. He tells us to have a good time.

Any remaining anxiety evaporates when we arrive at the

114

designated pickup place. For a start, there is more than one minibus, and each of the three sports the same logo. Backpacking twenty-somethings flit back and fore to a shop, encouraged by the radio-blasting drivers to stock up on bottled water. It is early morning in early January, but already the temperature is touching twenty Celsius.

As we reach the city limit, leaving the ancient red walls and general cacophony of Marrakech behind, our driver gives a little respite from the radio and introduces himself. His name is Osama. 'But don't worry,' he says, 'I'm not like that other one.' It's a shame he has to excuse himself through humour. I'm not sure how popular the name Osama is in the Arab world, but I wonder how it has fared since 2001. I don't know that there are many Adolfs in Germany, or anywhere else, these days. But the joke has dismissed any awkwardness in his bus full of mainly young Westerners. Clearly, we are not being kidnapped.

As the road snakes up toward the snowy peaks of the High Atlas, the mountains that provide the stunning backdrop to Marrakesh and form the last barrier to the Sahara, Osama teaches us the Arabic for 'Go-go-go!' – '*Yallah-yallah-yallah*!' – encouraging us to shout for him to put his foot down as we career ever more dangerously around hairpin bends and looping rollercoaster curves. The shouting is fun, but soon worried glances dampen our collective enthusiasm for quite so much *yallah* up the side of a mountain.

Below the precipitous drops that lie just beyond the toy-town crash barriers, we glimpse traditional Berber villages. Just a few miles beyond the modernity of Marrakesh, life goes on as it has done for centuries. Donkeys are piled high with goods being moved from village to village, and one begins to glimpse the chain economy that ends in the souks adjacent to Djemma el-Fna. We start to pass little roadside stalls selling decorated plates and tagines; sometimes there are rugs that lend credence to many a carpet salesmen's boast that 'it's all Berber work', a guarantee of quality.

The mountain road is an umbilical cord to civilisation, hinting at an ancient way of the world that has been thinly disguised by the structures of Western capitalism. The poor of the rural hinterlands sell to mobile traders who sell to merchants in the city who sell to tourists. All the way to the desert, we are still in the grip of a well-oiled capitalist machine. We stop at designated places where we are escorted into the most expensive restaurants.

By the time we reach the second or third such tourist trap, a solidarity has grown up amid a group who realise that although we are not being kidnapped for ransom, we are being taken for a ride by a loosely affiliated network of businessmen who are likely exploiting the local craftspeople as much as they are attempting to squeeze every last dinar from our pockets. An unspoken pact emerges, to unfollow the guides and seek out cheaper food outlets and less sophisticated commercial operations. We buy our souvenirs from haggard-faced Berber men lurking quietly behind stone walls, their only sops to marketing ragged cloths on which their wares are unevenly spread.

At Ait-ben-Haddou, the complex of casbahs on the main caravan route out to the desert, we give in and purchase some drawings coloured in the traditional style, experts holding paper over a flame until the cobalt-blue skies and saffron-yellow sands are revealed as background for a quick further squiggle from which Picasso-esque camels emerge, half-hearted Rocinantes of the Sahara.

After a guided tour of the impressive *ighrem*, a fortified village that has played host to the filming of dozens of movies – including biblical epics, James Bond films, a clutch of Scorsese classics as well as modern blockbusters like *Gladiator*, *Kingdom of Heaven* and *Prince of Persia* – we are escorted back to the minibuses. As Ait-ben-Haddou disappears into the distance, it is odd to reflect on how this one collection of earthenware structures, not one dating back beyond the seventeeth-century, has provided half of humanity with its vision of antiquity. As far as we movie-goers are concerned, this is ancient Egypt, ancient Persia and ancient Rome rolled into one with ancient Greece, ancient Israel and the odd bit of actual Maghreb. It's a classic case of Orientalism, where all things 'Eastern' look the same under Western eyes. A desert is a desert is a desert.

The Draa valley soon puts paid to this misconception, its shimmering ribbon of river snaking through a series of lush oases below the N-9 road out of Ouarzazate. Elaborate irrigation has allowed the region to become the date basket of Morocco, as well as harbouring the intensive cultivation of henna, fruit trees and vegetables.

As dusk falls, the date palms fade into the rear view mirror. Ahead lies Zagora; after that, only sand. There is time, however, for one final stop, where Osama hands us over to a rum looking bunch of Tuareg tribesmen in full desert headwraps. We are told we need water and at least a scarf for the desert, to shield our eyes and mouths from the wild winds that will whip up the sands. The feeling among the group is becoming mutinous. No more will we be told what to buy and where to buy it. An American couple walk off in search of an alternative shop from which to purchase their water; a local businessman shrugs, knowing they have a better chance of being eaten by vultures.

Out in the desert, a degree of communality is engineered through the international language of music. Our guides begin by beating a drum, and then adding another couple of traditional instruments into the mix. It soon becomes clear, however, that they are much better at guiding camels than they are at singing. As the night-time desert temperatures plummet and the Saharan sky affords a glimpse of the heavens, even the primal appeal of the cursory campfire cannot turn our minds from cwtching in bed.

Then, suddenly, the Tuareg nomads produce a Spanish guitar. The one with the blue headwrap flashes a gap-toothed grin and plucks a couple of flamenco sounds before beginning to strum something everybody knows. *Me gusta aviones, me gustas tu, me gusta viajar, me gustas tu.* The Spaniards especially go into raptures, whooping loudly and springing to their feet. Predictably, they like the bit about marijuana. It must be said, the Tuareg seem to like it, too.

Africa's Quiet Revolution

Buea, 2013

In the front room of a large brick house in the village of Tole, surrounded by the tea plantations of South-West Cameroon, a group of women who call themselves Charity Sisters close their regular meeting with a special song. Music is in the lifeblood of Africa, and in a semi-literate society, the power of song to hold individual emotion and collective memory is underscored by its simple communicative power. The lyric of the Charity Sisters' anthem, like the slogan on their plastic chairs – 'Charity Sister's Ass' – is simple and direct. 'Women have a role to play,' they sing.

The song – and the group – encapsulate Africa's Quiet Revolution: the empowering of women. The second verse celebrates the work of Omam Esther, Executive Director of the small Non-Governmental Organisation Reach Out Cameroon, whose work we are here to witness with a view to setting up a partnership under the Wales for Africa programme. Esther and her team work out of a humble office in Bakweri Town, a central district of nearby Buea (*boy-ah*), a university city of some 200,000 people and the administrative centre of the South-West region, one of the Cameroon's two Anglophone Sub-Divisions.

'Reach Out have a role to play,' the song continues, 'we thank you God / for giving us Esther / Reach Out have a role to play.' It is easy to understand why the Charity Sisters group, established in 1993, are overjoyed at their own partnership with Omam Esther's NGO. Put simply, Esther is a force of nature, one of those strong

119

women leaders who commands in all those she meets equal measures of admiration and trepidation. Her own staff, including daughters Lundi-Anne and Bibiche, call her 'Madame Esther' or, more usually, simply 'Madame'.

The day before our visit to Tole, we travelled with Madame Esther, under escort of the Cameroonian military's Rapid Intervention Battalion (B.I.R.), to the disputed border territory of Bakassi, where Esther delivered a speech as powerful as it was audacious. Quoting Martin Luther King's 'I Have a Dream' is perhaps the ultimate expression of hope for a better future, and despite that it might be bordering on passé in the West, its resonance at a Public Hearing for Women, in the presence of the Canadian High Commissioner, Benoit-Pierre Laramee, and Kofi Awity, head of the EU's programme to support Civil Society efforts in the region, is more than clear.

Even the Cameroonians are privileged to be here. Bakassi is two days travel from Buea – on roads so poor and dangerous that even the journey is more a hope than an expectation. Few urban Cameroonians venture out into what are commonly referred to as 'The hinterlands'. 'NGOs,' Esther informs us, 'don't go there.' It is easy to understand why. Along with its inaccessibility, the oil-rich peninsula has for decades been a territory disputed between Cameroon and neighbouring Nigeria. The International Court of Justice took eight years, using documents dating back to the Scramble for Africa and particularly Anglo-German agreements in the 1880s, before finally ruling that Bakassi is indeed a part of Cameroon on October 10 2002, a decision ratified by the UN.

Although direct conflict between the nations has ceased, there are still huge residual problems in the area. Many Nigerians have found themselves unwilling citizens of Cameroon and Cameroonians have felt intimidated by the large Nigerian populace in the area. Already poor, much wealth creation that does happen in Bakassi benefits communities in Nigeria rather than the local people. Rapes and kidnappings are still frequent. If it were not for the efforts of Reach Out – and, it must be said, the support of the Canadian High Commissioner – the people of Bakassi would be conveniently forgotten by the rest of Cameroon, let alone the wider world. Lombat K., the commander of the troops charged with our safe passage through the mangrove swamps of Africa's inside corner, jokes that he would rather be fishing, like so many of the poor people whose basic huts line the muddy banks of the Akwegafe River, rather than 'fishing out the Canadian High Commissioner'. The Commissioner laughs in agreement. It is, as in the aftermath of any conflict, a desire for the return of normality that dominates the thoughts of those concerned.

But things cannot be put back exactly as they were. As the day wears on, the unrelenting temperature and humidity sapping the last vestiges of our energy, it becomes ever more clear that the High Commissioner, the EU representative and even the military acknowledge that the answer to Bakassi's complex problems lies partly in Esther's simple solution, chanted like a mantra amid the chaotic din that greets our arrival at the public hearing: 'Women working for women to build a sustainable peace'. We are, all of us, having made it through the forbidding, pirate-infested waters of the Gulf of Guinea – which under Western eyes look for all the world like a scene from *Apocalypse Now* – to show support for Esther and her cause. His Excellency is the guest of honour; he makes a speech of his own, but when he does it is Esther who holds his microphone. It is an impromptu gesture of practical support, but in the pictures – and on Cameroon's national TV network – it comes across as highly symbolic.

Set against song, the speeches seem a dry formality. Working tirelessly with women's groups in this remote community, Reach Out Cameroon workers have taught the locals an anthem. 'Women of Bakassi / woman is peace' is its simple refrain – celebratory, inoffensive, but unapologetically political. It is also reminiscent of the Charity Sisters back in Tole. When the tribal elders and Sub-Divisional commanders take the floor they use the opportunity of meeting the High Commissioner to emphasise the importance of security, pointedly failing to mention women at all. Later, they are happy to throw money at the dancing girls whose raucous performances follow the speeches; it is a sight reminiscent of a lap-dancing club and underlines the present state of affairs. Where women seem mobilised to embrace a new mode of being in the future, the men who stand to lose most from such a quiet revolution doggedly hang on to the unsatisfactory past.

En route to Bakassi, despite the best efforts of the B.I.R. to steer a course through the dark shallows, we twice ran aground on the treacherous shelves of sand that lurk beneath the water. Everybody remained calm – charity workers, visiting teachers and the ambassador all waited patiently for the troops to do their job. The media attempted to film the delay and were firmly told to put their cameras away. Each time we stopped we were underway again in less than half an hour, but one could sense the tension among the troops. A silence descended that spoke volumes about the genuine danger we might have been in had the engines not been revived and the boats rescued from the more innocuous peril of low tides, as if the maximum security arrangements and the boxloads of heavy ammo had not already rammed the point home.

But the fact we got going again after such an impasse in the circumstances seems somehow symbolic. As we make up for lost time, wind rushing through our hair as we speed through the maze of rivers that criss-cross the peninsula like veins, women *are* being empowered. Field studies show that female genital mutilation, once widely prevalent among the tribes of this area and described by one charity worker as 'fashionable', is in steady decline. This is still a society riddled with rape, incest, child trafficking and other abominations, but a consciousness has taken hold. Education is beginning to have an effect. And it is only by standing together that women can face down the perpetrators and those who would use the veil of conflict to turn a blind eye to such flagrant human rights abuses. It is thanks to the work of Omam Esther and Reach

Out Cameroon that the women of Bakassi know they are not alone.

It is not just within the high stakes world of international diplomacy that Reach Out Cameroon is having a quiet yet profound and measurable impact. Spending a day following Esther around Buea and its environs takes in the Father's House Orphanage, run by Comfort, a woman living with HIV who had been ostracised within her community. Reach Out installed her at Father's House, generating the double impact of a loving mother figure for vulnerable children and a new lease of life for Comfort herself.

From the orphanage we travel by jeep to the first of two Muslim women's groups; the first meets at a humble dwelling in a nondescript neighbourhood of huts and shacks, the second in a large brick building across the road from Buea's largest mosque, on the misty slopes of volcanic Mount Cameroon, whose hazy outline dominates the town. Muslims are a marginal minority in the predominantly Christian country, but Cameroon is characterised by a rare religious tolerance and despite Esther's own unshakeable Christian faith, her drive to 'reach out' and work with society's most vulnerable members means that she has forged as strong a bond with Muslim women as she has with their Christian counterparts. Love and respect are in evidence wherever she goes. Each group receives Esther and her party with its own brand of rapturous welcome.

Between visits, and the inevitable 'chop' that accompanies each (African culture demands that we are fed and watered at each stop along the way), Esther is constantly on her mobile phone, making and answering calls in a bewildering mix of English, French and Cameroonian Pidgin English. Her tinny ringtone is the somewhat incongruous 'Boom Boom Boom' by The Outhere Brothers. Pidgin, the local *lingua franca*, however, suits Esther's *modus operandi*. A hybrid born of colonisation, its mix of English and local tribal languages is characterised by a vernacular directness and grammatical structures that to the untrained ear seem mangled out of all sense. There is no masculine or feminine distinction and a lack of euphemism; when a lady wishes to take a comfort break, the request is recycled as 'He want piss.'

This directness runs right through Cameroon. This is a country with a life expectancy of fifty-one and an economy too small to accommodate its twenty million inhabitants; there is never enough money to go around and the marginalised are inevitably doomed to scratch an existence rather than a life. With the ever-present spectre of poverty, and death lurking not far behind (funerals are big business in Buea), life on the streets is vibrant and joyful. People live for the moment. Afrobeat pop blares from every window and doorway, speakers turned up so loud that the sound quality is distorted; car horns and cockerels add to the cacophonous soundtrack of communities crowded with street-hawkers on the make and the ubiquitous humidity and dust.

Back in Tole, another group of women gather around a wooden table and offer us 'chop'. This time it is doughnuts, dried fish and Coca-Cola. The doughnuts are the delicious result of yet another Reach Out training programme – the Keep a Girl Alive project – and part of a micro-business venture that the girls can call their own. Over and above the practical assistance, however, the 'sustainable development' now accepted as so crucial to any kind of aid work, the major benefit of the charity's intervention is clear to see.

The girls are visibly uncomfortable with meeting Western visitors asking questions about their lives. It is hard not to wonder how low-burning a sense of self-esteem can become before the flame flickers out altogether. Some of the girls talk vividly, passionately, extolling the virtues of the Reach Out project and the training they have received. Emotion runs high; the girls are clearly grateful. But even the relatively outgoing members of the group rarely smile. The quieter ones can barely summon a word in English or in Pidgin; only under duress do they whisper their all-too-similar tales of having dropped out of school at Primary level, their parents no longer able to afford the fees, and having 'put to bed' (Pidgin for giving birth) at 'tender age'.

But somewhere in these whispered tales of lives still in process of being turned around there beats a louder drum. The KGA Girls' stories are an echo of those we have heard elsewhere. For the first time in scores of generations, Africa's women are being listened to – and being heard. In Tole, and in Buea, and in Bakassi, women are beginning to work for women – and to work for themselves. Africa's Quiet Revolution will not happen overnight; it lacks the web-literate savvy of the Arab Spring and the media-friendly theatricality of Occupy, but it may nevertheless come to shape the twenty-first-century world more profoundly than either.

Canaan Happyland

Small Soppo, 2013

> Oh, my sister, did you come for help to me?
> Pray and give me your right hand
> Oh, the land I am bound for
> Sweet Canaan's happy land
> **Spiritual**

You wanted an African church. You wanted music and dancing and colour; you wanted to see joy. I needed an African church. I needed straight talking and integrity and simplicity; I needed to see God.

Julie had prepared breakfast. In the simple pair of apartments rented by Reach Out Cameroon for its volunteers, we sat down to a feast of fresh fruit the like of which I had never seen. In this part of Buea, the water supply is only turned on in the morning of every third day and there are frequent interruptions in the electricity supply, but the bananas and watermelon and pineapple are unsurpassed.

After breakfast, we wondered if we were suitably attired. How smart should we be? How much covering up was appropriate for you? This was a poor community, but there was a high degree of dignity and respect. I opted for the smartest clothes I had with me: blue suede shoes, grey formal trousers and a collarless dark blue cotton shirt I had acquired in India, which seemed made for the circumstances. You got changed at least twice before settling on a white chemise that at least covered your shoulders. Julie approved, in the end.

We walked through the village, Small Soppo, past children playing in shabby T-shirts. We followed Julie, who was walking quickly. Time, as we had discovered, worked differently here; but still, there was a distinct sense that we were, if not late, then pushed to meet a prior appointment. Arriving, we had to scramble up a small bank. From outside, the building looked like it might have been abandoned. Fashioned out of grey concrete breezeblocks, the church was indistinguishable from the houses that surrounded it. There was no street name to lead you to it, nothing to make the building stand out, not even a sign outside.

Entering the single room of the tin-roofed hut, it seemed as if the congregation had been waiting for us. There was a small row of plastic chairs free at the front, within spitting distance of the barely elevated stage. Julie escorted us to these seats and then turned on her heel and took a place nearer the back. On the seat was a well-thumbed Bible.

Where two or three are gathered in my name,
there am I in the midst.
Matthew 18: 20

The service began with a message. Maybe they had been singing and praying until we arrived. Maybe it was always like this in Cameroon. Maybe we were simply late. Pastor John was smartly but humbly attired; a shirt and tie, grey waistcoat and pinstriped trousers had a touch of the West about them. Conditioned to be embarrassed about the colonial past, I felt a little uncomfortable when we said we were from Britain to be greeted with the claim that 'this is your country'. It was in fact a warm welcome, tempered only by the fact that there is a movement in South-West Cameroon to secede from the Francophone dominated remainder of the country. But Pastor John was not at Canaan Happyland to talk about politics. He was here to deliver, in a clear and uncompromising way, the gospel of Jesus Christ.

I had grown up in a Christian household, and thought I knew the gospel. Jesus died to save us from sin. Because we were born sinners, we deserve to die, but by grace He died in our place. I knew the theory. I had, a long time ago, accepted the reality. But I had got lost along the way, like those seeds in the Parable of the Sower that get stolen by the birds or fail to germinate in the stony ground. For a long time I had equivocated the gospel with the postmodernism I had acquired at university and the liberal-left values I had accepted via the *Guardian*. It was a worldview without recourse to truth, adopted in the same unquestioning manner for which I might well have criticised a 'religious' person.

In the process I had forgotten – or, perhaps, I discovered, I had never known – for example, the difference between morality and righteousness. I had shared with you, on the backseat of the minibus the previous evening, on our return from Bakassi, my reservations about Christianity. This business of morality was at its heart.

One by one, Pastor John took my concerns, my reservations, my genuine questions about both the veracity and doctrine of Christian teaching, and knocked them down. Righteousness, I learned, is not the same thing as morality; righteousness is a gift from God. If I want to be moral, and here the pastor drew on an example very close to me – alcohol – I can make a decision. I can give up drinking alcohol to avoid being led into sin. But this is a moral decision; and such moral decisions alone cannot make me righteous. I had believed in a moral universe that did not necessarily depend on God, but I realised all along the contradictions inherent in such a view. Without a universal judge or arbiter of what is right and what is wrong, human beings are free to construct their own moralities, much as the postmodern liberal-left has done. No one means badly by constructing a code by which to live that has at its core a compassion for all human beings and a determination that all forms of human prejudice must end. There is little that is unbiblical in the UN Declaration of Human Rights. But meaning well is not an entrance ticket to the Kingdom of God. Moral relativism can only take you so far.

The second big problem I had was Paul. I could, I told you, totally accept Jesus, or – at least – the teachings of Jesus as they are recorded in the gospels. The disciples called Jesus 'Rabbi', which means 'Teacher', and the lessons of the self-styled 'Son of Man', were for me reassuringly vague. Jesus talks mainly in riddles, or at least in parables and allegories that many people fail to understand. He left a lot open to interpretation. Although He was direct and sometimes harsh, He would very rarely condemn outright. Where He did so, the target of his ire was usually a figure that would also be a target for the liberal-left: tax collectors, the rich, and above all religious leaders. To revisit the gospels after a long period of not reading the Word, it is startling to discover just how much of Jesus' ministry is spent rebuking Pharisees and Saducees.

And this was my basis for a lack of faith in the Church. I could accept Jesus, but often my own experience of church – to include all human attempts to live out a Christian life – had been less than impressive. My childhood had bequeathed me squabbling and petty infighting, politics and money-grabbing as the hallmarks of organisations that professed Jesus. Magnified by the media, things were even worse, and the bigger the organisation, the worse it got. The Church of England is, to many people of my political persuasion, nothing more than a misogynistic, homophobic lobby group; its Catholic counterpart not far short of the world's biggest paedophile ring. Of course these things are not true when seen from a decent distance and fair-minded perspective, but the church is also its own worst enemy.

I blamed Paul. To my mind, the man responsible for most of the New Testament had taken the words of Jesus – probably the Son of God, and certainly an excellent teacher of ethics – and made a religion out of them. I told you as much on the minibus from Bakassi. I did so earnestly and without wishing to disrespect the beliefs that you held dear. For the first time in a long time, I genuinely wanted to know, to learn, perhaps even to believe. It was my first time in Africa and I desperately wanted to know what it was that they had here that the West seemed to have lost.

Here, even the taxis carried Biblical slogans. Verses were everywhere in a way that back home would have seemed somehow anachronistic. In Wales, such scriptural omnipresence is associated with a bygone era and with a vague sense of sombre oppression. Maybe it is partly because we only ever see such images in black and white that chapel-going Wales is associated with the idea that the only concession to gaiety was a striped shroud. Here in Cameroon, everything was in technicolour. Taxis are bright yellow, presumably in homage to New York, but are generally 'pimped' to include fluffy dice or their equivalent, windshield decals and numerous other stickers, often proclaiming Jesus.

To my eyes, the churches were different too. The huge variety of Protestant denominations represented again felt like Wales might have done a hundred years ago. Christianity here seemed more authentic. It seemed like all the things I wanted it to be. All the things I told you on the minibus when you asked me what my ideal church would be like. Grassroots, bottom-up. Time and again in the gospels, Jesus characterises the Kingdom of Heaven as a kingdom of the poor. It had taken Cameroon to make me realise that I didn't really have a problem with God. It was Church as institution – as hypocrisy, as dogma – with which I had developed a problem. Here was a poor, imperfect country, riddled with corruption and socio-economic deprivation on a scale that makes the use of such a phrase in a European context seem like an insult, and yet here also were the followers of Jesus.

When you had asked me to describe my perfect church, what I had unwittingly described was Canaan Happyland. I could not possibly have known that Julie's church would be the way that it was. It was not what you were expecting from an African church. There was no thronging horde of people dressed in bright colours.

Jesus Christ. The same yesterday, today and forever
Hebrews 13: 8

This was text that adorned the first church building I ever attended regularly, and it was replicated here at Canaan Happyland. Here was a church I recognised; not a supranational institution habitually bringing the faith into disrepute in the eyes of the world, simply a small group of believers doing their best to live by faith. And this type of church, I had to admit, the type I felt comfortable with, was exactly like those encouraged by Paul.

Each of Pastor John's points – and he drew heavily on Paul – hit home like arrows to my heart. I had been primed by the Holy Spirit to receive God's Word and here it was, relentlessly joyful and uncompromising. The preacher leapt around, evidencing the truth of his sermon all over Old and New Testaments. As my fingers worked through the pages lightly, flicking between Matthew and Hebrews, Ephesians and Chronicles, I remembered how well I knew this book; only its import had been neglected. As I did so, I could sense you in the seat next to me, leaning over to share the readings, quietly impressed.

As I began my journey back to faith, one of the ideas I had toyed with was the familiar idea that all roads might lead back to a very vague concept of God, some kind of universal life force. The Abrahamic faiths – Judaism and Islam, as well as Christianity – were all, surely, subjects of a tragic misunderstanding; their belief systems seemed bound up in each other. And plenty of other ways of understanding the world, from Buddhism to socialism, made their own kind of sense. But even these multiplicitous, accommodating waves of thought were dashed on the rocks at Canaan Happyland.

First a young woman with scars on her neck got up and gave

testimony: how she was in a relationship with a Muslim man who saw their difference of faith as an excuse to violently abuse her, physically and emotionally. She spoke with such passion about how she felt God was telling her to follow His own will by seeking out a Christian partner that we could not fail to be moved. But the drama was not in the violence of the story – sadly, that could have happened in any relationship, whatever the combination of faiths or not – rather in the way it was relayed. Despite the young woman's horrendous injuries – this boyfriend had attempted to strangle her with a piece of wire – and the very much present emotional legacy, she spoke only with love about the perpetrator. She wanted for him the same thing as for herself, the chance to follow his faith and find a like-minded partner. There was no condemnatory bitterness, no blame attached to another belief system, only the failure and fallibility of a single human being. This, to me, was Christianity in action; this girl had turned the other cheek.

Then came the moment I had felt in the deepest places of my soul had been coming all along. Much later, you told me that I fairly leapt onto the small stage. It was then that you saw something in me. Potential, you called it. Something God could work with, something you could love. All I wanted to do at the time was profess. Testify. God knows I had grown up in churches where personal 'testimony' was at the heart. Stories of what God had done in the lives of individuals were a constant feature. But nothing – nothing like this – had ever happened to me. My story – my testimony – started only when I began to drift away from God. I had grown up with drama all around me, but not *my* story. That was what you called it, later; this is *your* story, you said, happy to have been both a witness and a key player.

It isn't an uncommon story. And it's only remarkable to me because it's mine. The Prodigal Son. God, the father in that story, welcomed me back with open arms. At Canaan Happyland, you could feel the joy in the room. I shook the pastor's hand and thanked him for having preached the Word of God. I told the congregation of how we had come to be there, setting up a link between our school and a charity, the fact that you were a Christian and I was not, a little of my own faith history. I didn't speak for long, but of the things that matter I had said everything.

Afterwards, we stayed behind – not for long – and the ministers prayed. Pastor John and his friend who had come down especially to preach as well that morning. You know the rest. I am only writing this down to commemorate, to freeze the moment in time, to attempt its capture, because that is what I do. The story's coda is the rest of our lives. After prayer, Pastor John delivered his simple vision. We both knew what it meant. We both knew, immediately, weirdly-wonderfully, that it was right.

> *They will be like a tree planted by the water,*
> *that sends out its roots by the stream.*
> **Jeremiah 17:8**

Two trees.

Acknowledgements

The pieces that make up this collection were written over a period of thirteen years. A huge amount of other writing, and life, has happened amid and between the experiences related here. Revisiting these pieces – some of which have previously appeared in magazines, anthologies and online, still others having been tidied up from various notebooks – has been an exercise in reminiscence as much as revision. I am grateful to the huge number of people who have crossed my path over the last decade and a half: friends and colleagues who have contributed directly or indirectly to the potted autobiography that lies somewhere in the blank spaces between these pages will know who you are.

More immediately, I must thank my editor Adam Somerset for his diligence, good humour and efficiency and the publisher, Richard Lewis Davies, not only for taking this project on, but for all that Parthian Books has done for English-language publishing in Wales over what is now a quarter century; the company has come a long way since 53 Colum Road, a short walk from the Humanities Building where I first met Richard as a creative writing tutor on my first degree. Parthian published *Next* (2006) from which the title essay is taken, and *Nu:2* (2011), where the Slovene pieces were published under the title 'Postcards from a Small Country'.

Many of the essays here first appeared in *The Raconteur* or *Wales Arts Review*, publications founded on love and no money by myself and Gary Raymond. I am pleased to see that Gary has taken the *Review* from strength to strength in the years since I moved on to edit *the welsh agenda*. Thanks are due to Lee Waters for welcoming me aboard the good ship IWA, to Jess Blair for her support as I cut my current affairs teeth, and to Auriol Miller, Rhea Stevens, Laura Knight, Shea Buckland-Jones, Barbara Powell and Merlin Gable who make my current role such a joy. 'Together, Stronger', 'Mexico: Dying for the Truth' and 'What Everything Looks Like From Here' were all first published on *Click on Wales*, the IWA's online platform.

Those with a good memory or a fondness for collecting obscure litzines may remember *CFUK*, the precursor to all of the above, from which 'Becoming Welsh in '99', 'Concrete, Steel and Sky' and 'Homage to Barcelona' are drawn. I must thank all those writers, and artists and photographers, who have contributed to the periodicals I have edited. Being Wales, this has been almost exclusively for love not money, and I have been both privileged and grateful to work with you all. The same goes for the indefatigable Sally Baker and the executive committee of Wales PEN Cymru; I hope we can continue the fight to make our country a place where literate, tolerant voices are heard loud and clear amid the din and darkness.

Further afield, I must thank Jasper Rees for commissioning work from Wales for *theartsdesk.com*. 'Making Hay in God's Own Country' was first published there. And of course, the Hay Festival itself has been a massive inspiration over the years, bringing some of the best in world literature and ideas to some fields in the small corner of Mid Wales I will always call home. It will be an honour to follow in the footsteps of my friend and mentor Jon Gower as Hay Festival International Fellow 2018-19, and I am indebted to

Peter Florence and his team for the opportunity. I very much hope the travel involved – to Mexico, Peru, Colombia and *mi favorito España* – might lead to another volume. Whether flying or driving, I intend on continuing to find beautiful fragments of home elsewhere, and in the lives of others.

Finally, love and blessings to my wonderful family – and to all the families of the earth.

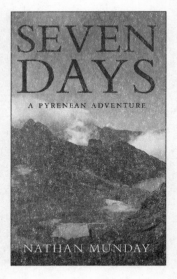

PARTHIAN

www.parthianbooks.com